D0854594

Adventurers in Buckskin

 *A TARGET BOOK*

Adventurers
in Buckskin

Edited, with commentary by Bennett Wayne

GARRARD PUBLISHING COMPANY
CHAMPAIGN, ILLINOIS

Picture credits:

American Museum of Natural History, New York: p. 43 (bottom)
The Bettmann Archive: pp. 47, 161
The Brooklyn Museum, Dick S. Ramsay Fund: p. 92
Carnegie Library of Pittsburgh: p. 50
Culver Pictures: pp. 131, 155, 158
Denver Public Library Western History Collection: pp. 33, 99
Gilcrease Institute of American History and Art, Tulsa, Oklahoma: p. 89
Joslyn Art Museum, Northern Natural Gas Company Collection, Omaha, Nebraska:
      pp. 16, 22–23, 43 (top), 44 (both), 45, 57, 58, 65, 69, 110, 117, 126
Kit Carson Memorial Foundation, Inc., Taos, New Mexico: p. 120
Library of Congress: pp. 72, 135, 142
Missouri Historical Society: p. 21
Montana Historical Society Collection: p. 125 (left)
Picture Collection, New York Public Library: pp. 39, 77, 82, 148, cover
Rare Book Division, New York Public Library, Astor, Lenox and Tilden Foundation: pp. 102, 107
Remington Art Memorial, Ogdensburg, New York: pp. 29, 124
Santa Fe Trade. Publication of the Gilcrease Institute of American
      History and Art, Tulsa, Oklahoma, 1965: p. 125 (upper right)
South Dakota Memorial Art Center. Painting by Harvey T. Dunn (1844–1952).
      Jedediah Smith in the Badlands. 1947. Gift of the artist: p. 9
The Trapper's Guide by S. Newhouse (New York: Mason, Baker and Pratt,
      1874): p. 125 (middle and lower right)

Acknowledgments:

From *When Mountain Men Trapped Beaver* by Richard Glendinning
(Champaign, Illinois: Garrard Publishing Company, 1967):
      "Buffler Comin'!"
      "The Amazing Alarm Clock"
      "Yellowstone Country"
      "Mount Hood Hijinks"
      "A Salty Story"
From *Bent's Fort: Crossroads of the Great West* by Wyatt Blassingame
(Champaign, Illinois: Garrard Publishing Company, 1967):
      "Felled by a Mountain"
From *Twenty Years Among the Hostile Indians* by Captain J. Lee
Humfreville (New York: Hunter and Company, 1903):
      "Sudden Death"

Copyright © 1973 by Garrard Publishing Company
All rights reserved. Manufactured in the U.S.A.
International Standard Book Number: 8116–4900–8
Library of Congress Catalog Card Number: 72–6741

Contents

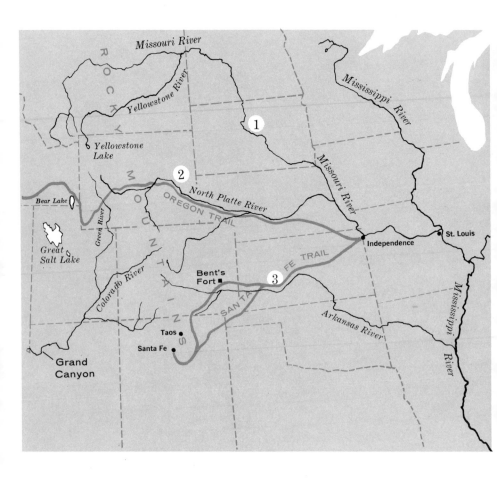

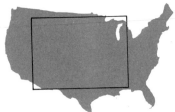

Mountain men of the early 1800s took one of two routes to the West: the river route (1) via the Missouri River to the present-day state of Montana, or the overland route (2) which came to be called the Oregon Trail. At various times mountain men also rode with traders on the Santa Fe Trail (3) to Mexican territory.

Destination — West!

This is a book about adventurers—about the daring men who headed West in the early 1800s to trap beaver in the Rocky Mountains. Some of them were hired by fur companies. Others worked alone. But all of them braved danger to find their way into the wide and unexplored spaces of the West. They sailed up the wild Missouri River by keelboat or rode across the dry and treeless plain in wagon trains. At the end of the journey were the towering Rocky Mountains—and adventure!

Let fearful men stay safely at home! Mountain men roamed freely under western skies—and faced danger every day. Many drowned or were clawed by grizzly bears. Others died of hunger or thirst or were killed by Indians. A mountain man had to be on guard every minute of the day and night!

When the few short years of the fur trade were over, most mountain men stayed in the West to hunt buffalo or scout for the army. Others led wagon trains across the wild and beautiful country they had made their own.

Within the pages of this book are the exciting life stories of four great westerners—Jed Smith, Jim Bridger, Kit Carson, and Buffalo Bill. Here are the Indians—those who were their friends and those who were their enemies. Here are tales about buffalo hunts, narrow escapes, and strange discoveries. Here, in short, is the West.

This historical collection can be read for information in the fields of literature and social studies. But, most especially, it should be read for pleasure!

JED SMITH
1798–1831

—greatest of the mountain men—
packed his Bible, shouldered his rifle,
and headed West with General Ashley's
band of fur trappers in 1822. Jed was
filled with a hunger to see and to chart the
wild and unknown places of the West.
Soon he was riding far and wide, first as
one of Ashley's men and then as one of
the partners of Smith, Sublette, and
Jackson. The trappers he led in search of
beaver became the first white men to
cross the Sierra Nevada Mountains from
west to east. They were the first to cross
the Great Salt Lake Desert, and the first
to travel overland from southern California to the Columbia River. Jed Smith
lived—and finally met his death—in a
world filled with danger and violence.

Jed Smith
Trailblazer and Trapper

by Frank Latham

Copyright © 1968 by Frank B. Latham

A Smell of Campfire Smoke

"Hey, young fellow! How about selling me some tobacco?"

Young Jedediah Smith dropped his book on the store counter. "Sorry, sir, I didn't hear you come in. You walk kind of quiet."

The man laughed. "It's a habit, young fellow. Where I come from, you walk quiet and look sharp. If you don't, the Indians will get you."

Jed carefully studied the man. He was tall and lean, with long hair and a bushy beard. He wore a fur cap and buckskin clothing. There was a smell of campfire smoke on him. No doubt about it—the stranger was a hunter.

Jed handed the hunter a package of tobacco. "Are you from the Ohio country?" he asked.

"Farther west than that. I've been up the Missouri as far as the Yellowstone River."

The man put a coin on the counter. Then he took a closer look at Jed.

"You're a big fellow," he said. "Soon you'll be heading West. Maybe I'll see you out there."

Jed's eyes glowed as he watched the man leave his father's store. He felt a hunger to go West. It was a hunger like wanting apple butter on a piece of fresh-baked bread.

In this year of 1809, Jericho, N.Y., seemed dull to Jed. Every day wagons left the small farming town as families packed their belongings and moved West. Jed wished his family were going too.

The Smith family had moved often. Jed's father had moved from New Hampshire to Connecticut, where he had met his wife. Later the Smiths had moved to New York State. Like many other families, they were looking for better land. They wanted to make a new start in life.

The door opened, and Jed's father entered the store. "Thanks for helping me, Jed," he said, smiling at his tall, dark-haired son. "Now I have another chore for you. Your mother says we need one more rabbit for the stew tonight."

"Good," said Jed happily. "I'll try to get one." He picked up his rifle and hurried away.

Stepping quietly as the hunter would have done, Jed walked across a meadow. Ahead of him he saw a rabbit nibbling grass. "Remember," Jed said to himself, "squeeze the trigger; don't jerk it." The rifle cracked. The rabbit leaped high in the air and dropped to the ground. Jed picked it up and took it home to his mother.

Jed liked to roam the fields and woods with his rifle. But he also helped his family with the chores. He sold sugar, flour, bacon, and other supplies in the store. He helped his older brother raise corn and potatoes and milk the cows. He carried water and split wood for his mother and his three older sisters.

Jed's mother had taught her children to read from the family Bible. Now and then a schoolteacher would stop in Jericho for a month or two. Every month a Methodist minister rode to Jericho to preach. He liked Jed and let him borrow a history book and a geography.

That night, after a good dinner of rabbit stew, the Smiths sat around the fireplace.

Jed's father was speaking of his family. He told about their moves to new land. "I have a feeling," he said, "that this family is not through with moving."

Jed looked into the flames and thought of the rivers the hunter had talked about. He dreamed of exploring them.

White Space on a Map

When Jed was twelve, his family did move. They went to North East Township in Erie County, Pennsylvania.

Here, young Jed met Dr. Titus Simons. He was the village doctor and also a scholar. Jed was eager to get an education, and the kind doctor lent him books. Dr. Simons and Jed often had long talks together.

One day, Dr. Simons gave Jed a book about the Lewis and Clark Expedition which had explored the Far West. Jed's heart thumped as he read about the explorers.

Jed hurried to see Dr. Simons the next day. "I've finished reading about the Lewis and Clark Expedition," Jed said excitedly. "I've looked at the map showing where they went. What about the country south of the Columbia River? There's nothing but white space on the map."

"The space is white because no one knows what's there," said Dr. Simons.

"I want to find out what's there," said Jed. "Are there mountains and rivers? Is there good farmland?"

"I've thought about that, too, Jed. Maybe you'll be the man to find out."

Several years later, Jed's family moved farther West. They went to Green Township, Ohio, not far from Lake Erie. Jed was happy when the Simons family moved to Ohio too.

Jed was eighteen now. He was six feet tall, and strong and lean. He got a job as a clerk on a Lake Erie freight boat. British fur traders, who traveled to and from the West on this boat, liked Jed. He was never too busy to help them write letters.

The traders talked to Jed about the fur business. "A man can make a lot of money trapping beaver," they said.

Jed was full of questions. "Have you ever been in the Rockies? What sort of land is south of the Columbia River?"

"I don't know much about that Rocky Mountain country," said a fur trader. "The man who goes there is likely to get scalped by Indians."

As Jed worked at his desk on the freight boat, the paper in front of him seemed to turn into a map. The map had white space on it. Jed would jump up and shake his head. "I've got to stop thinking about that country. I see a map every time I look at a piece of paper."

When Jed was 22, he made up his mind to leave for the West. Jed had five younger brothers now. He hoped to make enough money trapping beaver to help educate the boys. Then he would have time to explore —he would find out what was in the white space on the map.

Jed went to say good-bye to Dr. Simons. The doctor handed Jed a book of hymns. "These hymns and your Bible will help you, Jed. You are going to a wild country. But don't forget your religion."

Jed gripped Dr. Simons' hand. "I won't forget. I want you to be proud of me."

Jed Learns His Trade

Dogs barked and people cheered as General Ashley's keelboat pulled away from the St. Louis dock. Jed Smith stood on the deck and looked eagerly ahead. West and north of St. Louis was the wilderness. It was May 8, 1822, and Jed was on his way to the land he had dreamed of seeing for so long.

Jed was one of more than 100 trappers General Ashley had hired to go up the Missouri River. A large party led by Major Andrew Henry, Ashley's partner, had left. Jed was in the second group.

Many of the men were greenhorns, and, like Jed, had never been trapping in the Far West. But there were several trappers who knew the mountains well. Among them were Moses Harris and Art Black. They were bearded men, who liked to joke and sing and tell stories.

The heavy keelboat slowly moved up the river. It was loaded with supplies and things to trade with the Indians. Moses, Art, and Jed went ashore to hunt. An elk ran across the plain about 50 yards away. Jed aimed and fired his rifle. The elk fell dead.

"You may be a greenhorn," said Moses Harris, "but you are a good shot."

"I was lucky," said Jed. But the praise made him happy.

Five months later, the men reached Fort Henry on the Yellowstone River.

Soon Ashley started back to St. Louis with furs that had already been collected. At the same time, Major Henry led a trapping party into the Big Horn Mountains. Jed went hunting with another trapper and then caught up with Henry's party.

The older men showed Jed the best places to set his traps. The men waded in the water while they worked so the beaver would not smell them and be scared away.

The first beaver Jed caught weighed about 40 pounds. Its silky fur was dark brown and its tail gray. Soon he caught others and skinned them. The pelts were then dried and pressed into large packs weighing 100 pounds. Later they would be loaded on horses and mules and taken to Fort Henry.

One day, Major Henry and Jed were walking together up a small stream, looking for signs of beaver. Suddenly Henry stopped and pointed to a leaf floating toward them.

"Get in the bushes," he said. "Lie down and keep quiet."

Jed did as he was told.

The two men lay still for many minutes. Finally Henry got up.

"What were you waiting for?" asked Jed.

17

Setting Traps for Beaver by Alfred Jacob Miller

"Indians," said Henry. "That leaf in the water might have been knocked off a bush by an Indian. The Blackfeet might have been upstream waiting for us. I guess I was wrong. But it's better to be careful than dead."

Thick ice began to form on the streams. The trappers built cabins and settled down for the long, cold winter.

Jed puzzled the trappers. He didn't drink whiskey, and he read books every day. He chopped a hole in the ice to get water to wash and shave. The men liked him, however. They agreed that Jed was a good trapper and a crack shot.

One morning, Jed heard running water. The ice was melting, and spring was coming. But suddenly tragedy struck. A group of Blackfeet raided the camp. Some of the trappers were killed, and many horses were stolen.

Henry led the men that were left back to the fort.

"We'll stay in the fort and wait for Ashley," said Henry. "He is bringing more men from St. Louis. They'll be a big help if the Blackfeet attack again."

"Someone ought to go meet Ashley," a trapper suggested. "Our men can't work without horses. Ashley can buy some for us."

Henry agreed and asked Jed to make the trip. Jed was pleased. He felt that Henry believed he was a man to be trusted.

The Battle with the Rees

Jed headed downriver in a dugout canoe. He met Ashley's keelboats where the Cheyenne River runs into the Missouri.

Jed was introduced to Jim Clyman, one of Ashley's most experienced trappers. He liked the tall, bearded man at once. Jim had a firm handshake and a friendly smile.

Jed told Ashley that Henry had lost most of his pack horses and needed more.

"The Ree Indians have horses," said Jim Clyman. "Their village is nearby. We'll have to try and trade with them."

Ashley nodded in agreement. The keelboats moved on up the river to the Ree village. The Rees had built a log wall around their lodges. "It looks as though they are ready for trouble," said Jim Clyman to Jed.

At first the Rees seemed friendly. But when the trading began, they were hard to please. The Indians didn't want beads and cloth. They wanted only powder and bullets.

"I don't like this," said Jim Clyman. "They'll soon be shooting those bullets at us."

Ashley just laughed. "You always expect trouble. Cheer up, Jim!"

By evening the trappers had nineteen horses. That

night, the horses would be kept on the riverbank near the Ree village. Then, Jim Clyman, Jed, and 40 men would take the horses to Fort Henry.

To keep the horses together, the men put rawhide hobbles around their front legs. With a hobble on, a horse could walk but not run.

The next day, there was a storm, and the men could not leave. Jim Clyman still expected trouble from the Rees. He warned the men to stay awake that night. Jed lay behind a log and stared into the darkness. Drums boomed steadily in the Ree village. Jed tightened his grip on his rifle and waited and waited.

Suddenly an owl hooted. Seconds later there was another hoot.

"That's a Ree signal!" shouted Jim Clyman. "They're going to attack!" There was a puff of smoke from the wall around the village as a rifle cracked. Then smoke poured out of the wall as the Rees opened fire. Horses screamed.

Jed ran to help the men guarding the horses. He told them to cut the hobbles. Then they could drive the horses into the river and let them swim to safety.

It was hard work cutting the hobbles from the frightened horses. Two men helping Jed were killed. Jed felt a bullet rip his sleeve.

"Jed!" shouted Jim Clyman. "Come here before you get killed! You can't save those horses!"

Jed hated to leave the helpless horses. But he knew Jim was right. The men ran to the river and dived in. Several men were killed as they swam to the keelboats.

The keelboats were moved downriver from the Ree village. The next day, Ashley called a meeting. "We'll go back down the Missouri to the Cheyenne River," he said. "I'll send a message to Henry and tell him to meet us there."

Ashley called for a volunteer to carry the message. Jed and Jim Clyman both stepped forward.

"Two men should go," said Jim. "It's 200 miles to Fort Henry. The country will be full of Indians."

Fur trappers on the Missouri often faced attack by hostile Indians such as the Arikaras.

"But I want you here, Jim, in case of trouble," said Ashley.

"I will go along with Jed," said Baptiste, a French-Canadian trapper.

Jed and Baptiste started off on foot. They hiked each night and hid from the Indians during the day. Several times Indians rode within 50 yards of them.

It took several weeks for Jed and Baptiste to reach the fort. Major Henry started off at once. His canoes moved swiftly down the Missouri. They drifted quietly past the Ree village at night and reached Ashley's camp safely.

A company of trappers on the trail. Some brigades carried their supplies in small covered wagons.

Ashley and Henry decided to give up the river route to the Yellowstone country. Instead, they would send small trapping parties overland into the Rocky Mountains. In the Rockies, the trappers could trade for more horses with the friendlier Crow Indians.

Each summer, the trappers would gather at a meeting place—a rendezvous. They would turn in their furs and get supplies for another trapping season.

Ashley had one more announcement. "Jed Smith has earned the right to lead a trapping party," he said.

Jim Clyman stepped forward and took Jed's hand. "I'll go with Jed Smith!" he shouted.

Moses Harris, Art Black, and a dozen other bearded mountain men gathered around Jed. They slapped him on the back. The men remembered how Jed had risked his life trying to save the horses. They remembered his 200-mile trip to Fort Henry. "Jed's our man!" they yelled.

Jed Fights a Grizzly

"Grizzly! Grizzly!"

At the warning shout, Jed Smith whirled in his tracks. He looked down the line of trappers he was leading.

Suddenly, a huge grizzly bear leaped on Jed. As he hit the ground, Jed grabbed his knife. The grizzly swung a paw tipped with razor-sharp claws. Jed felt a sharp, savage pain in his side. He plunged his knife into the grizzly.

Now Jed found himself looking into the grizzly's mouth. He twisted away, but the bear's jaws struck the top of his head.

Blood filled Jed's eyes. But he kept on swinging his knife.

Dimly, he saw the grizzly towering over him. Jed thought he heard the crack of a rifle. He was on his knees swinging his knife when he heard Art Black's voice.

"Take it easy, Jed. I killed the grizzly."

Jed was dizzy with pain. His head was on fire, and his side ached like a bad tooth.

"Thunderation!" shouted Dave Jackson. "That grizzly nearly took Jed's scalp off, and did it as slick as a Blackfoot! Almost took his ear off too!"

"Get some water. Let's wash him off and see what we can do," said Jim.

Jed tried to sit up. He started to fall over, but strong hands gripped his shoulders.

"Jim," he said, "get a needle and thread. You've got some sewing to do."

Jim sewed up the cut running from Jed's left eyebrow across his forehead. Then he sewed Jed's scalp and left ear back in place. Jed gritted his teeth and clenched his fists till his hands ached.

Jim took off Jed's ripped and bloody shirt. He felt his ribs and found that several were broken. He wrapped a piece of buckskin around Jed's body.

"Jed," said Jim, "if that grizzly's paw hadn't hit your bullet pouch, you'd have been dead."

"I guess the good Lord is looking after me," said Jed. "I must thank Him in my prayers."

That night, Jed lay by the campfire and read his Bible. Then he said his prayers and rolled up in his blanket. His friends watched in surprise and wonder.

"Jed is a strange one with his Bible reading and praying," said Dave Jackson. "I've never seen another man like him in this country. But he is a MAN!"

Through South Pass

Jed and his men spent the winter of 1824 in a Crow Indian camp in the Rocky Mountains. The Crows were friendly and glad to have company.

The wind howled day and night. Snow piled high around the skin lodges. Jed soon got restless. He kept looking at a map of the Rockies.

The Indians called them the Shining Mountains. They talked about a pass through the Rockies, which were then largely unexplored. Jed wanted to find the pass.

In February Jed led his men out of the Crow camp. It still was bitterly cold. But Jed would not wait for warmer weather. He was eager to find that pass.

The men traveled through what is now southern Wyoming. Before long they ran short of food. There was nothing to shoot. The birds and animals were under cover because of the cold.

The streams were frozen solid. For drinking water, the men had to melt snow. In the Wind River Range, the wind was so strong that it blew away their campfires.

Then, one day, the weary men reached a broad opening in the saw-toothed mountains. "We're in the pass!" they shouted.

They danced a little jig of happiness. Jed had found the one place through which wagons could cross the Rockies. In years to come, thousands of settlers would go through South Pass to California and Oregon.

On the western side of the Rockies, the land was full of beaver. "They are just sitting around waiting for us to catch them!" shouted Art Black.

In a month, the trappers had many furs. Jed told three men to take the furs back to General Ashley. He led the other men northwest to explore new beaver country.

Into the Unknown

The trappers' rendezvous in the summer of 1826 was in a valley near Bear Lake. This lake is on the border of today's Utah and Idaho. Men from all over the West gathered at the rendezvous.

Jed, though only 27, now commanded 70 of Ashley's trappers. Major Henry had retired. During the rendezvous, Ashley told Jed he wanted to retire too. He offered to sell his fur business to Jed, Dave Jackson, and Bill Sublette.

The three men accepted the offer. Then they sat

down to make plans. They agreed that Sublette and Jackson would lead the trapping parties. Jed would explore new beaver country.

Jed hurried away to his tent to study his maps. Southwest of Great Salt Lake was an unknown land. There was a big white space on the map. Jed wanted to fill in that white space.

Jed left Bear Lake with seventeen men. He missed Jim Clyman, who was now living on a farm. But faithful Art Black was with him.

The men rode southwest through a country of sand and bare hills. The hot sun beat down on them every day.

Many of the rivers the men crossed were nearly dry. Soon horses and mules began to die from lack of grass and water.

When the men reached the Colorado River, they crossed it and then rode along its bank. The men were worn-out and half-starved. Several begged Jed to turn back.

"We must keep going," said Jed. "I promise you we'll reach an Indian village soon."

In several weeks, the hungry men did indeed reach a Mojave village on the Colorado River. They all shook their heads in amazement.

"Now how in thunder did Jed ever know we'd find a village so soon?" asked one of the men.

"Jed has a feeling for the country," said Art Black. "Those eyes of his seem to see through mountains."

The Mojaves fed the trappers and traded horses for beads and cloth. Jed's men rested, then crossed the Colorado again and started westward through the wild Mojave Desert. It was hotter and drier than the land they had already crossed. Soon Jed's tongue felt like a chip of wood. But he kept going, and his men followed him.

They were now in California, which was then owned by Mexico. Soon they had to climb the snow-capped San Bernardino Mountains. The men were so

Jed Smith and his men crossing the Mojave Desert

tired that they kept falling down. But even so, Jed would not let them turn back.

Finally they reached the top. They saw a green valley and sparkling water ahead. Jed knelt and thanked God for helping him to lead his men to safety.

Jed went to see the governor of California. But the governor was not happy to see Jed. What was this hunter doing here? Was he a spy? Were the Americans planning to take California from Mexico?

Jed told the governor that his men were trappers. They wanted to buy supplies and go back home. "May we go north to Oregon and then back east?" he asked. "It would be easier than going through the Mojave Desert."

"You may buy supplies," the governor finally said. "But you'll have to go back the way you came." He didn't want Jed to see any more of rich California.

In January the trappers started east. But when they neared the Mojave Desert, Jed turned north. "I'm not going to risk my men's lives crossing the desert," he told Art. "I think the Lord will forgive me for disobeying the governor."

Before long they entered the San Joaquin Valley. The great Sierra Nevada Mountains towered to the east. The valley was full of deer, bear, and beaver. The men stopped to trap some of the beaver.

At the Stanislaus River, Jed built a camp. He decided to leave most of his men there. He would hunt for a pass through the mountains. He promised the men he would return to the camp in California on September 20.

On May 20, 1827, Jed, Robert Evans, and Silas Gobel started east. Although it was May, the snow in the mountains was from four to eight feet deep. Howling winds battered the men. Two of their pack horses died.

It seemed almost impossible to find a pass. They would go up a trail and then see high cliffs blocking their way. Three times in one day they had to turn back. But on the fourth try, they found a pass! They were the first white men to cross the Sierra Nevada Mountains from west to east. The trip had taken them eight days.

Now the sun-baked deserts of Nevada were ahead of them. As they pushed on and on, their eyes ached and their throats burned with thirst.

When they reached the Great Salt Lake Desert in Utah, Robert and Silas could barely walk. Jed urged them on. He wondered how long he could keep going. Four horses died and were eaten by the men.

One day Robert fell to his knees. "I can't go on," he gasped. Jed dug a hole in the sand. He buried Robert up to his neck in it.

"This will protect you from the sun till I can get some water," said Jed.

"There is no water anywhere," mumbled Robert.

Jed and Silas took a kettle and started walking. Where, where was there any water?

Then, a few feet ahead, they found a flowing spring! Jed wanted to drink and drink, but he knew that too much water would make him sick. He wet his forehead, and then bent over the spring and drank deeply. He and Silas filled the kettle and went back to give some to Robert.

Robert soon felt strong enough to walk to the spring. They rested there for one day, then started walking again. In eight days, the ragged, hungry men reached the rendezvous at Bear Lake. The trappers looked in amazement at Jed, Robert, and Silas. It was hard to believe that they had really crossed the Great Salt Lake Desert. No other white men had ever done it.

Back to California

Ten days after reaching Bear Lake, Jed started packing to return to California. He had promised his men that he would be back by September 20. He was tired, but he meant to keep his promise.

Jed left Bear Lake with eighteen men. He followed a somewhat different trail than he had used the year

Trappers and Indians shared in the serious business of trading and in the rowdy fun at rendezvous.

before. Within a month, the trappers reached the Mojave village on the Colorado River. The Mojaves acted just as friendly as they had a year ago. But secretly they were getting their bows and arrows ready.

Several months earlier, a party of trappers had killed several Mojaves. They were waiting for a chance to kill some white men. Their chance came when Jed's men were getting ready to leave the village.

Jed and eight other trappers began to ferry their supplies across the river on rafts. The rest of the men and the horses waited on the riverbank for their turn to cross.

Suddenly, John Turner, one of the trappers with Jed, shouted, "The Mojaves! They're killing the men on the bank!"

Jed saw showers of arrows falling on the trappers. Turner aimed his rifle.

"No!" said Jed. "It's too late to help them. Save your bullets for later."

Somehow, Jed and his men managed to paddle their rafts to the far bank. "We're in a bad fix," said Turner. Jed nodded. They had only five rifles. All the men on the other side of the river had been killed, and all the horses had been stolen.

Quickly Jed ordered his men to build a wall of branches and logs to hide behind. They watched the Mojaves cross the river and creep toward them. Two Indians were nearing Jed and his men ahead of the others.

"Take the one on the right," Jed told Turner. "I'll take the other one. If we hit them, it may scare the others off for a while."

The rifles of both cracked, and both Mojaves fell. The other Indians howled and ran back to the river as fast as they could go.

Jed saw his chance. "Hurry, men! Get your packs, and let's go!"

Jed kept his men marching all night. The next morning they found a spring. They stayed there all day and then started out again. They had no way of carrying water, so when springs were far between, Jed cut up cactus. He had the men chew the pieces. "Cactus juice isn't as good as water," he said. "But it will keep you going."

At last they reached the San Bernardino Mountains. Slowly they struggled over the top and into the valley where water was plentiful. Jed bought food and horses at a ranch. Then he led his men to the camp where he had left his men in May. They reached it September 18.

"We knew you'd get back," one of the trappers cried. "But we didn't expect you to be here ahead of time!"

Trouble in Oregon

Jed had to have supplies for the trip back east. Again he went to see the governor of California.

The governor was angry when Jed walked into his office. But there were some American ship captains in California. They talked to the governor and calmed him down.

The governor finally let Jed buy supplies and travel north through California to Oregon. This was a long way home, but an easier route than the ones they had used before.

Jed and his men trapped beaver as they traveled north along the river now called the Sacramento. At first the traveling was easy. Then they entered a region full of fallen trees and thick brush.

Jed sent men ahead with axes to cut a path. During ten-hour periods, the trappers seldom traveled more than two miles.

Hostile Indians now began following them. Every few minutes, Jed would hear the zip-zip-zip of arrows. In five days, six men were wounded. Jed moved up and down the line of men to urge them along.

"Close up!" he shouted at them. "Don't lag behind! If you do, you'll be killed by Indians!"

The men turned west and cut across to the Pacific Coast. They stayed close to the beach, and the Indians stopped following them. They pushed north again and were soon in Oregon, where they camped by a river to rest.

The Indians in Oregon came into camp to trade furs for beads and cloth. They seemed friendly, but Jed warned his men to be careful.

The very first day in camp, things went wrong. A trapper saw an Indian steal an ax. The men grabbed the Indian and forced him to give the ax back. Jed tied him up to give him a good scare, and then let him go.

The next day the men moved on to another camp. The following morning, Jed, Richard Leland, and John Turner went off to find a trail. Before they left, Jed warned his men not to let any Indians into the camp.

Jed, Leland, and Turner spent the morning blazing a good trail. As they were returning to camp by canoe, Indians fired on them from the riverbank. Bullets whistled over their heads. The three men paddled quickly to the far bank and ran.

Later they circled back and climbed a small hill. From there they could look into the camp. Tears were in Jed's eyes as he turned away. The Indians had killed every man in the camp. His heart felt like a stone when he thought of Art Black.

Three weeks later, they reached Fort Vancouver, a trading post on the Columbia River. It belonged to the Hudson's Bay Company, a British trading concern. Jed was overjoyed to find Art there—alive! Art had run into the woods when the Indians began to attack the men.

The trappers spent the winter at Fort Vancouver. Early in the spring, Jed and Art started back east. Turner and Leland stayed at Fort Vancouver. Before long Jed and Art joined the other members of their trapping company in the Rocky Mountains. Then they began hunting beaver again.

The Last Trail

"There goes Jed Smith. He got rich trapping beaver. Now, he's retired and lives on a farm near here." The man spoke loudly to his friends. He was proud that such a famous man lived in St. Louis.

Jed Smith hurried down the street. He didn't like to hear people talking about the money he'd made. He was more interested in the trails he had blazed.

Now he was writing a book to tell people about the wonderful country west of St. Louis. He also was working on his own map of the Far West.

Of course, it was good to have money. He was able to help his parents and his brothers. Two of his brothers, Austin and Peter, were living with him. He also had sent gifts to his good friend, Dr. Simons.

Jed had reached St. Louis in October 1830. His last year of trapping had been a good one. Then he and Dave Jackson and Bill Sublette decided to sell their fur business.

Now, six months later, Jed was getting restless. He had talked to traders who took wagons down the Santa Fe Trail to Mexico. They said the Mexicans wanted to buy cloth, pins, needles, buttons, and other goods.

Jed had never been to Santa Fe. He wanted to see this part of the country so he could finish his map of the West. He talked things over with Dave Jackson and Bill Sublette. They decided to organize a caravan of wagons and go to Santa Fe. Jed's brothers, Peter and Austin, would go with them.

The caravan left from Independence, Missouri, in April of 1831. The trip was an easy one until they reached the Arkansas River. Then they faced a 60-mile stretch of desert.

There were no rivers and just a few water holes in this lonely land. With good reason, the Mexicans called it "the journey of the dead."

Jed rode at the head of a wagon train such as this one heading across the desert to Santa Fe.

Jed and his men soon found that "the journey" would be more dangerous than ever. There had been little rainfall. The water holes they found were all dry. Savage sand storms began to whip them. The flat, sun-dried land seemed to stretch on forever.

Within a week, the caravan ran out of water. Men began to ride wildly across the desert searching for water holes. Two men never came back. On May 27, Jed spoke to Dave and Bill.

"Calm the men down," he said. "Tell them I'll go hunt for water. I have a feeling that it's near."

"This is like old times," said Dave Jackson. "Once more, you are going out to find water. You found it in the Mojave and the Great Salt Lake Desert. I'm sure you'll find it here."

Jed smiled. "I'll need some luck. If I don't come back tonight, don't wait for me. I'll see you in Santa Fe." Jed rode away.

' The caravan pushed on and found a water hole that evening. The men waited for Jed to join them, but he did not return.

The worried men marched on to Santa Fe. There was no trace of Jed. No one had seen him. Suddenly, Jed's brothers ran up to a Mexican trader. "That rifle! Those silver pistols! Where did you get them?" They were Jed's weapons.

The trader said he had bought them from Comanche

raiders. The Indians told him they were at a water hole when a white man appeared. He calmly rode toward them, making the peace sign. But suddenly an arrow hit him in the shoulder. He killed two Comanches before he fell. There were a dozen arrows in his chest. He was a brave man, they said.

No one knows where Jed Smith died. No stone marks his grave. But he wrote the names of many rivers and mountains on the maps.

Jed Smith was the first white man to find South Pass. He was the first to travel from the Missouri River to the coast of California. He was the first to cross the Sierra Nevada Mountains from west to east. He was the first to cross the Great Salt Lake Desert. He was also the first to travel by land from southern California to the Columbia River.

A brave and fearless leader of men, Jed Smith lived to complete his dream of filling in the white spaces on the map.

41

About Trappers, Indians — and Artists

Most of the Indian yarns told by mountain men around a dying campfire were of daring battles and narrow escapes. Grizzled old trappers outdid one another in their tales of stolen horses, of Indians on the warpath, of scalpings and revenge.

Mountain men, alone and unprotected in the wilderness, did indeed have to be on guard against unfriendly tribes. For the most part, though, old hands in the fur trade lived peacefully with the Plains Indians. From Mandan and Sioux and Snake and Cheyenne, they learned how to survive in the wild country—how to hunt buffalo, how to preserve food, how to keep warm. They wintered in Indian villages. They shared their rendezvous with the red men. Often they married Indian women. Some of them even became Indian chiefs!

The world of the Plains Indians has been painted by several artists—George Catlin, Alfred Jacob Miller, Charles Bodmer—who ventured into Indian country with bands of trappers during the heyday of the fur trade. They shared the rugged life of the trappers and were witness to a way of life that would soon disappear. Their sketches and paintings from life are a priceless record of the Plains Indians of the early 1800s.

A Gallery of Plains Indians

These proud Indians of the West . . .

Painting by Alfred Jacob Miller

. . . lassoed wild horses and rode them magnificently.

Painting by George Catlin

. . . lived as nomads, roaming the plains with their families.

Painting by Alfred Jacob Miller

. . . hunted the mighty buffalo with lance and arrow.

Painting by Charles Bodmer

. . . fought their enemies with courage and daring.

Painting by Charles Bodmer

. . . honored their chiefs, such as this Minnataree warrior.

JIM BRIDGER
1804–1881

was only eighteen on the fateful day in 1822 when he sailed up the Missouri River with General Ashley's fur-trapping expedition. As an apprentice in a St. Louis blacksmith shop, Jim had listened to the talk of mountain men and dreamed of the day that he, too, could head West. And now the day had come! Jim trapped for Ashley, rode with Jed Smith, and finally became an independent trapper. He lived through hair-raising adventures fighting Indians, sailing down the seething Bear River in a bullboat, and exploring the wonders of the Yellowstone country. Jim was always ready for a scrap—and always ready for a good story too. He became known far and wide for his yarns and his tall tales, which often turned out to be closer to fact than to fiction!

Jim Bridger

Man of the Mountains

by Willard and Celia Luce

Copyright © 1966 by Willard Luce and Celia Luce

Squirrel for Supper

"Jim! Where are you, Jim?"

Young Jim Bridger was aiming his gun at a squirrel on the fence rail. Slowly he squeezed the trigger. Then there was a loud bang.

Only afterward did he answer his sister's calls.

When she reached him, Jim held up the three squirrels he had caught that morning. "Squirrel for supper," he announced proudly. "I'll skin them as soon as we get home. Maybe ma will make you some gloves from the hides, after I tan them."

Jim's sister beamed with delight. Suddenly she remembered why she had come out looking for him. "If you don't hurry home, ma will more than likely skin you. There are three carriages at the inn for you to clean. And there are horses to feed and water."

Jim frowned. He liked to hunt, and he didn't mind too much working on the family farm. But he hated the thousand and one chores around the inn that his father and mother also owned.

"Why in tarnation do people have to stop this early in the day?" he asked.

He broke into a run, knowing he had a lot of hard work to do.

The year was 1812, and the place was Richmond, Virginia. Everyone seemed to be moving, or wanted to move, West. People talked about the new land there —rich land, cheap land. They even joked about how rich it was. They said you could plant seeds one minute, and then the next minute you had to jump out of the way because the seeds sprouted and grew so quickly.

People also talked about the wild animals. They told of huge herds of buffalo, elk, and deer. Thousands of beaver lived in the cool mountain streams just waiting to be trapped.

Whenever Jim Bridger heard these tales, he got a tingling of excitement down his spine. More than anything else, he loved to hunt and trap. He wanted to see the animals and places he had heard so much about.

To Jim's surprise, Mr. Bridger had an announcement to make that very night. The Bridgers were gathered around the table, eating squirrel for supper. "Children," Mr. Bridger said, "your mother and I have decided to move West. We are selling our farm and inn here. We will be going as soon as we can get ready."

Young Jim Bridger let out a shout of joy. It might have been heard as far as the "Shining," or Rocky, Mountains.

Jim Bridger's family floated down the Ohio on a flat-boat like thousands of other families that emigrated to the frontier in the early 1800s.

Moving West

Mr. Bridger bought a covered wagon. All the family's possessions were loaded into it. Then they started West. There were five of them: Mr. and Mrs. Bridger, young Jim, his sister, and a baby brother.

Jim liked traveling. "Look at those bear tracks!" he shouted, pointing at the side of the trail.

"What bear tracks?" asked his sister. "You're always seeing things that no one else sees."

"Look out!" warned his father. "When you are driving, you are supposed to watch the road."

"Yes, sir." Jim pulled the team back onto the rough roadway. "But a bear went past here not long ago. I'll bet he's right back there in the woods."

Finally they came to the Ohio River. Mr. Bridger sold the wagon and bought a flatboat. They loaded their belongings on the boat and continued their journey to St. Louis. Mr. Bridger bought a farm across the Mississippi River in Illinois. The place where the Bridgers settled was called Six Mile Prairie.

The next few years were happy ones for young Jim. In winter he set out traps and sold the furs from the animals he caught. In summer he worked on the farm. He fished in the river and hunted in the woods. Sometimes he helped the ferrymen carry passengers, wagons, and animals across the wide Mississippi River.

During this time he grew tall and strong and self-reliant. Then things changed. Mrs. Bridger became ill. Four years after coming to Six Mile Prairie, she died. Mr. Bridger's sister came to care for the family. Soon after this, Jim's little brother died, then his father.

Jim was no longer just a member of the family. He was now head of it. They needed money, and Jim was the only one to earn it.

"I know how to run a ferryboat," Jim said. "That's what I'll do."

Although he was not yet fourteen, Jim handled the ferry from Six Mile Prairie to St. Louis. He carried pigs, sheep, cattle, horses, wagons, and machinery.

The hours were long and the work was hard, even for a man. It took all Jim's strength to pole the ferry over the water. His muscles ached all night.

After a few months he had a chance to work in a blacksmith shop in St. Louis. Here men had iron shoes put on their horses. They had traps made and farm machinery fixed.

Learning to be a blacksmith was hard work too, but Jim liked it. His boss, Phil Creamer, was a friendly man and a good teacher. Jim loved the sizzling sound the hot iron made when he pushed it down into a barrel of water. This made the iron hard. Jim also liked to listen to the people who came to the blacksmith shop.

Sometimes trappers who had been to the western mountains came. They told of the beaver ponds and the thousands of beaver.

"How would you like to be a trapper, Jim?" one of them asked him. "There's money in beaver pelts. There's a big call for them now, here and in Europe. They use the pelts for those tall hats so many men are wearing."

"There would be plenty of excitement, Jim," another trapper said. "Why, on one trip I saw grizzly bears as big as horses!"

"Yes," Jim Bridger thought, "it would be great to be a trapper." The money he would earn could send his little sister to school. Jim had never had time for school. He could neither read nor write. But he wanted his sister to have an education.

There was no trapping expedition starting out right then. But Jim was determined to join the next group heading West.

Jim's Big Adventure Begins

One day Jim Bridger rushed into the blacksmith shop waving a newspaper. He spread the paper out on the bench and pointed to an advertisement. "Mr. Creamer!" he called. "Come here and read this to me! Please, won't you, Mr. Creamer?"

Phil Creamer rubbed his hands on his leather apron and leaned over the paper, peering at the small print. He read this ad from the Rocky Mountain Fur Company:

TO

Enterprising Young Men

The subscriber wishes to engage ONE HUNDRED MEN, to ascend the river Missouri to its source, there to be employed for one, two or three years. —For particulars, enquire of Major Andrew Henry, near the Lead Mines, in the County of Washington (who will ascend with, and command the party) or to the subscriber at St. Louis.

Wm. H. Ashley

"Mr. Creamer, do you think they'd take me to trap beaver with them?" Jim's blue-gray eyes were sparkling.

The blacksmith smiled. "Well, Jim, I reckon there's one way to find out."

"How, Mr. Creamer?"

"Ask General Ashley."

The ad asked for young men. Jim was young,

only eighteen. He was almost six feet tall. Five years of blacksmithing had hardened his muscles.

At first Ashley and Henry thought Jim was too young to be a trapper. But finally they decided to take him along.

On a spring day in 1822, the expedition was ready to leave. Jim's aunt and sister came to the landing to see him off. Phil Creamer and his family were there too. It seemed to Jim Bridger that everyone in St. Louis was there to bid the expedition good-bye.

One big keelboat was loaded with supplies and men. The other keelboat would follow in a few weeks.

Horses for the men to use were herded along the shore. Then Major Henry gave the command for the keelboat to move. Boatmen pushed on long poles. The people on the shore yelled and cheered. The men of the expedition shouted and fired their guns.

Jim Bridger looked back. There were his aunt and sister waving. They were all the family Jim had, and he was leaving them. There was Phil Creamer who had been like a father to him. He would probably not see them again for a long time. There was a stinging in Jim's eyes. He turned and looked upriver so no one would notice.

Fort Henry

Day after day the keelboat slowly crept up the Missouri River.

Jim Bridger spent most of his time on land. There he helped herd the horses. He shot rabbits and game for food. He explored the streams and prairies.

At last they came to the Indian village of the Arikaras, or the "Rees."

That day the Rees were friendly. Jim and some of the others traded trinkets for buckskin jackets, shirts, and trousers. Along with Indian moccasins, these became the "uniform" of the mountain men.

On and on they went. The sun grew hotter. Jim wondered if they would ever reach the Rocky Mountains.

August came, and a group of Assiniboine Indians rode up to join the trappers. They showed great signs of friendship. However, at the very first chance, they raced away with all the horses.

Jim never forgot this. From then on, he waited until he knew Indians well before he trusted them.

Finally the expedition reached the mouth of the Yellowstone River, 1,800 miles from St. Louis. Major Henry said, "Here's where we'll build a fort."

Jim Bridger looked around him in disappointment. Along the river there were cottonwood and

Mountain men trading trinkets for supplies in a Plains
Indian village in the West

Where the Yellowstone meets the Missouri, Jim saw only barren country (painted by Charles Bodmer).

willow trees. Beyond, there was only the rolling prairie covered with sagebrush. Where were the Rocky Mountains he wanted to see?

Many men had already deserted the company because the work was too hard. Jim was the youngest man there, but he was used to hard work. As the trappers built cabins and a fort, he did his full share. It was only a small fort, but it gave them protection from storms, wild animals, and Indians.

As the weather grew colder, the men started trapping. The new men, or greenhorns, were paired off with experienced trappers.

Jim Bridger's partner showed him how to set beaver traps. They started out their first evening. Each man carried six five-pound traps, a rifle, powder, shot, and a skinning knife.

Young Jim groaned under the load. "Tarnation," he grumbled, "I feel more like a pack mule than a trapper."

They reached a small stream and followed it. A beaver had built a dam of sticks and mud across the stream. This had backed up the water into a small pond. The beaver's house, or lodge, was near the center. It was a round dome of sticks and mud.

"Now, Jim," the old trapper said, "you wade out there and set your trap the way I told you. Set it near the beaver's lodge."

Jim stepped into the icy water. Before he had waded a dozen steps, he was shivering. By the time he had set the trap, he was shaking from the cold. He wondered if he would ever get warm.

Early the next morning, Jim and his partner set out to check their traps.

Jim waded out into the pond. The old trapper built a small fire on the bank and waited there.

Jim reached the trap. He peered down through the still water. There, almost at his feet, was a drowned beaver. Jim Bridger was shaking from excitement now.

"Hey!" he yelled to his partner. "We've got one!"

As he leaned over and reached down for the beaver, he slipped on a mud-covered limb, hidden under water. *Splash!* He plunged into the icy stream headfirst. Gasping and sputtering, he struggled upright. But in his hands he held a full-grown beaver.

He tried to call out, but he was too cold, too excited, and too wet.

"Now that's just fine, Jim," his partner said without any show of surprise. "You just bring him out here, and I'll show you how to skin him. Be sure to save his tail. Beaver tails are the best eating a man can get!"

Before Jim had a chance to get much more beaver fur, the second keelboat in the expedition arrived at Fort Henry.

Major Henry sent for Jim Bridger. "Jim," he said, "you've been a blacksmith. There's a blacksmith's outfit in the boat. Get it ashore and set it up in one of the cabins. Then you can make metal hinges for our doors and fix the traps and guns that are broken."

Jim nodded, in his serious-minded way. He had come up the Missouri River to be a trapper, not a blacksmith. But, if blacksmithing would help the Rocky Mountain Fur Company, he was willing to do it.

Through South Pass

Jim Bridger spent the next winter in the Big Horn Basin of Wyoming. The Crow Indians there were friendly, and the trappers camped with them.

One day Jim was led to a large tepee. A fire burned in the center. Around the fire sat many chiefs of the Crow nation. For some time they stared silently at Jim. He stared back, looking from one unsmiling face to another.

The fire threw strange shadows on the tepee. Jim licked his lips and swallowed hard. He wished someone would speak.

Finally Jim spoke up, "Even the wind talks more than the Crows."

"Yes," a chief nodded, "but the Crows want to make Jim Bridger a brother. The wind does not." With this, the chief smiled. The others smiled too. All at once, everyone started to talk and laugh. Then the ceremony went on, and Jim was adopted into the Crow tribe. His Crow name was *Casapy*, which meant "Chief of the Blankets."

By now Jim was almost 20 years old. His skin was tanned. His muscles had filled out, and he no longer looked so skinny.

In February Jedediah Smith led a small brigade of trappers from the Crow village. Jim Bridger was among them. They wanted to find a way to the Green River, which was on the other side of the Rocky Mountains.

They went southward and entered the Wind River country. As they climbed higher, the wind blew harder and harder. Jim Bridger pulled his beaver cap down over his ears. He clutched his buffalo robe and leaned into the wind. It was so strong he could hardly walk against it.

At last they reached more level country. There was very little shelter now. The icy wind screamed around them. They were too cold and tired to go any farther.

Jim Bridger pointed to a small thicket. He tried to yell, but the wind blew the sound away. Then he saw the others nod. All of them turned and staggered into the clump of trees. They huddled together to keep out of the wind as much as possible.

They tried to build a fire, but the wind was too strong. The men stayed in the thicket for two days without any food, without any fire, and without getting much sleep.

Once Tom Fitzpatrick, one of the trappers, poked Jim. "We'd better walk around a bit, Jim. We'll freeze to death if we don't." He had to yell to be heard above the wind.

The two of them staggered to their feet. Then they stumbled about in the darkness to get their blood circulating. But after a short while, they crawled back into the thicket. Never in his life had Jim Bridger been so cold.

Then during the night, the wind died slowly down. The trappers built a fire. Jim felt warmth creep back into his body. They cooked meat from a mountain sheep someone had shot. Jim Bridger ate his fill. Then he rolled in his buffalo robe and went to sleep.

The next morning they went on. Sometime near Jim Bridger's twentieth birthday, March 17, 1824, they crossed through South Pass.

Jim looked around him. To the north the tall peaks of the Rocky Mountains were jagged against the sky. To the south there were badlands. "What a discovery!" he said to himself. "In the summer wagons could go through here without very much trouble."

Jim was right. It was the easiest way through the mountains. Within 25 years, covered wagons by the hundreds would be rolling through South Pass and on to Oregon country.

Jim's eyes glowed as he looked west. Ahead were thousands of miles of unknown country. He picked up his rifle and moved forward.

Discovery of Great Salt Lake

Six months later Jim Bridger was with a group of trappers in northern Utah.

The trappers had just finished supper. The campfire was warm, and the talk was low and easy. "You know," one of the men said, "I'd surely like to know where that crazy river goes." He nodded toward the Bear River flowing softly by the camp.

Some thought it went into the Green River. Others insisted it went north to the Snake River.

"Maybe it goes clear to the Pacific Ocean," said Jim.

The men argued. Jim decided to find out for himself.

The next morning he started to build a bullboat. He made the boat from willow limbs. He stretched fresh buffalo hides over the limbs and fastened them down. Then he sewed the hides together tightly. He melted some buffalo fat and poured it over the seams. This made the bullboat watertight.

It was not a beautiful boat. It looked like a big tub, and it was hard to handle. But it would take Jim Bridger where he wanted to go.

Into the bullboat went Jim's rifle, some powder, shot, and a supply of dried buffalo meat.

By now Jim Bridger wasn't quite so sure he

Trappers gathered around the evening campfire told
strange tales and planned daring adventures.

wanted to go down an unknown river all by himself. But no one else offered to go along. He stepped
into the boat and pushed it away from the bank.

The trappers waved and yelled out their good-
byes. Jim waved back.

At first it was easy, riding the smooth water. After
a while, he heard the voice of the river grow louder
and stronger.

Jim thought of stopping and scouting ahead. Then
it was too late. The rushing river sucked him into
a canyon. The rough water bounced and whirled
the bullboat around. It smashed the boat against the
huge boulders. Jim was sure it would be knocked
to pieces.

Then, suddenly, the boat shot out of the canyon. Quickly Jim poled the boat ashore.

He climbed the steep canyon wall. The river ran to the southwest. In the distance he could see an open valley and mountains. Carefully he looked for Indian signs. There were no tepees, no smoke from campfires, and no dust from traveling feet.

Still Jim was not satisfied. He climbed higher. At last he could see a long shimmer of silver. Jim decided it was a lake.

Then he went back to the bullboat. He poled it down the Bear River. Finally he came to the lake. The sun made him thirsty, and he reached over the side of the boat and scooped up a handful of water.

As soon as he tasted the water, he spat it out. "Salty!" he roared, almost choking. "Tarnation! It's salt water! This must be the Pacific Ocean!"

He stared about him in amazement.

Before long Jim rejoined his trapping brigade. Captain John Weber called out to him, "Well, Jim, have you been to the Pacific Ocean and back already?"

"I surely have," Jim announced. The trappers stared at him in disbelief. Then Jim held out his hand. "Here's a bag of salt to prove it."

The men crowded around. They stared at the salt, and then they tasted it.

Then one of them said, "I'll be a pollywog's uncle! It is salt!" A huge grin spread across his whiskered face. "Won't this taste good on beaver tails tonight! I'm getting mighty tired of using gunpowder for salt!"

A roar of approval went up from the other trappers.

In the summer of 1826 Jim Clyman and three of his fellow trappers sailed completely around Jim's "ocean." What Jim Bridger had discovered was not an arm of the Pacific Ocean. It was Great Salt Lake.

Surprises

After the long, cold winter of trapping, Jim Bridger was glad to see spring. Now he could explore new country and find new beaver streams.

During the summer he and a small band of trappers set out to explore the area that is now known as Yellowstone National Park.

As Jim rode up to one of the geysers, it hissed steam. Jim's horse reared up.

"Whoa!" Jim Bridger yelled, pulling on the reins. "It's nothing but a puddle of hot water!"

The geyser hissed again. The water suddenly shot high into the air. Jim's horse turned and tried to run away. "Whoa!" Jim yelled again.

Jim stared at the geyser, hardly believing what he saw. "Tarnation," he whispered to himself. "No one will believe this when I tell them. Why, the water shoots up taller than a flagpole!"

When they came to the mud pots, Jim's horse tried to run away again. Jim listened to the plopping sound of the mud as it bubbled. He stared at the colors and scratched his head. "You reckon this is where the Indians get their war paint?" he asked a trapper.

"I'm not sure," the trapper answered. "I've been told the Indians are afraid to come here. They think it's evil spirits making all those noises."

Late in the year 1830, Jim Bridger and his trappers left Yellowstone to explore southward. Finally they came to the Bear River again and followed it down to Salt Lake Valley.

Here they spent a peaceful winter, trapping and hunting. Then one night in March, a band of Bannock Indians surprised them. The Indians raced away with all 80 of the trappers' horses.

For a while the trapper camp was in an uproar; then Tom Fitzpatrick took charge. "We'll get those horses back," he said. "We'll have to walk, but we'll get them."

"I'll go," said Jim Bridger. Other trappers stepped up too.

"Take dried meat, a buffalo robe, and plenty of powder and shot," Fitzpatrick told the men.

In a short time 40 trappers started through the snow. All day they walked northward. And all night they shivered under their buffalo robes.

Five days later they found a large Bannock Indian camp. Close by were 200 to 300 horses, closely guarded.

"There they are!" Jim Bridger said.

Tom Fitzpatrick nodded. "Jim, you take half the men. Get as close as you can to the horses. I'll take the other men. When we charge the camp, you scare the horses. Run off as many as you can."

Roving bands of Indians often stampeded trappers' horses while the weary mountain men slept.

Quietly Jim led his men toward the horse herd. Where there was little sagebrush, they crawled on their hands and knees so that the Indians would not see them.

At last there was no more cover between the trappers and the horses. Jim Bridger motioned his men to scatter out.

Lying flat on his belly, Jim carefully aimed his rifle at one of the Indians herding the horses. He took deep breaths to keep his hands from shaking.

Suddenly there came a crash of rifle fire from the Indian camp. Fitzpatrick's yell could be heard above the uproar.

Jim Bridger squeezed the trigger of his gun. Leaping to his feet, he yelled as loudly as he could. He raced at the horses. The trappers followed him, all yelling and waving their rifles.

The horse herd whirled about in confusion. Jim grabbed a pony's mane and swung himself onto the animal's back. Other trappers mounted too. They raced the horses to a safe place, then stopped to rest. All the trappers were there. Luckily no one had been hurt.

"We came off with more horses than we lost," Jim Bridger grinned. "According to my count, there are about 120 ponies in this herd. Those extra 40 horses should pay us for our five days' walk."

Two Arrows

As the years went by, Jim Bridger found himself taking part in other Indian battles. In Indian country he always traveled carefully. He watched the ground for tracks; he watched the wild birds and animals. Whenever they were frightened, he tried to find out why.

One day Jim and a group of trappers met a band of Blackfoot Indians. The Indians waved a white flag of truce.

Jim Bridger and Tom Fitzpatrick watched the Indians. All the trappers waited with their rifles ready.

"Looks like they want to powwow," Fitzpatrick said.

Jim nodded. "But they're Blackfeet. You can't trust Blackfeet." Jim turned to three trappers. "Go out and see what they want. We'll cover you."

The three trappers left their weapons and walked slowly toward the Indians. Three Indians came to meet them. The six men stopped to exchange greetings and smoke the peace pipe.

Suddenly the wife of a trapper rushed across the grass and threw her arms around an Indian brave. She was an Indian, and this was her brother.

Excited talk came from the Blackfeet.

Jim Bridger rode forward. He sat tall and straight, his rifle across his knees. His eyes were narrow and his face stern as he watched the Indians for any sign of trickery.

A Blackfoot brave rode forward too. He held an arrow in his bow, ready for trouble.

Chief Sun, the head of the tribe, moved up to the side of Jim's horse. Jim Bridger cocked his rifle. At the sound, the chief reached out and grabbed Jim's rifle by the barrel. He tried to tear it from Jim's hand. The rifle exploded. The bullet thudded harmlessly into the ground.

As his horse reared and twisted about, Jim heard the twang of a bowstring. Pain slashed his back like a burning knife. He grunted as he tried to hold on to the rifle and the horse.

Then another arrow hit his back. Suddenly his

Peacemaking on the prairie. Just in case of trouble, rifles are at ready!

gun was ripped from his hands. The stock of the gun crashed against the side of his head. He was knocked from the saddle.

Almost as in a dream, he saw Chief Sun jump on his horse and ride away. Faintly he could hear the banging of rifles and the whir of arrows.

When the battle ended, Jim Bridger still lay where he had fallen with two arrows in his back.

"Jim," Tom Fitzpatrick said, "if I don't pull these arrows out, you'll go around the rest of your life looking like a porcupine. This is going to hurt."

Jim grunted, "Go ahead and pull."

Tom pulled, but the arrows wouldn't come out. "Here, Jim," said Fitzpatrick, pushing a piece of rawhide between Jim's teeth. "Bite down on this, and I'll try again."

As Jim bit into the leather, Fitzpatrick pulled with all his might. Jim groaned through his clenched teeth. Suddenly the arrow came out.

Fitzpatrick went to work on the other arrow. He removed the shaft, but the arrowhead would not budge. For three years Jim Bridger carried the three-inch arrowhead in his back.

Then he met Dr. Marcus Whitman, when the trappers gathered for their yearly rendezvous, or get-together, in the Green River Valley of Wyoming.

"Doctor," Jim said, "I've got an arrowhead stuck

in my back. It gives me a lot of misery. You reckon you could cut it out?"

Dr. Whitman nodded and got his instruments ready.

Jim lay on the grass. Trappers and Indians crowded around to watch. They had no medicine to kill the pain.

"Are you ready, Jim?"

Jim nodded. "I reckon so."

Marcus Whitman took up his knife and started cutting. It took a long time, but at last the arrowhead came loose. Now Jim was rid of the last of the two arrows.

Changes

Soon after this Jim Bridger married. His wife was the daughter of a Flathead chief. Her name was Cora.

"Have you ever been to the Yellowstone country?" Jim asked her. "Have you seen hot water shoot up in the air higher than that pine tree over there?"

Cora shook her head.

"Good!" Jim laughed with happiness. "We'll go there on our honeymoon."

When they started out, all Jim's trappers went along. Cora's father and some Flathead Indians went along too.

"This is a heck of a honeymoon," Jim grumbled.

"When you marry an Indian, you marry her whole tribe."

But he didn't really mind. Cora was a wonderful wife. She went with him and his brigade up and down the beaver streams. She took care of the tepee and mended all Jim's clothes. Most important, she made him happy. His joy was complete when their daughter, Mary Ann, was born.

But things were not going well in the fur trade. Tall silk hats were replacing those made from beaver hides. The price of beaver furs went down. Besides, there were few beavers left to trap.

Many of the mountain men were leaving the mountains. "Better come with us, Jim. The time of the fur trade is over."

But Jim Bridger stubbornly shook his head. "Not for me," he said.

But his old trapping partners were right. The days of the fur trade were coming to an end.

Other things, however, were happening in the Rocky Mountains. Dr. Marcus Whitman and his family had gone on to settle in Oregon. Each year a few more wagon trains made the trip over the mountains, on their way to Oregon or to California.

One day Jim saw his first big wagon train. Guiding the train was his old pal, Tom Fitzpatrick.

The two trappers hugged each other and danced

around like a pair of youngsters on the last day of school.

Before the wagon train moved on, Jim asked Tom if he would take six-year-old Mary Ann to Marcus and Narcissa Whitman in Oregon. "Tom," he said, "I want Mary Ann to have book learning. Marcus said he would teach her when she got old enough."

When the wagon train pulled out, little Mary Ann Bridger stood in the back of a wagon. Tears rolled down her cheeks as she waved good-bye.

Jim hated to see her go. But he knew times were changing. Book learning was becoming more important. He wanted Mary Ann to have the schooling he had missed.

Fort Bridger

The following summer Jim saw more and more wagon trains creaking across the plains. The Indians saw them, too, and became more warlike. They didn't want to lose their hunting grounds to the white men.

But Jim knew the settlers would keep on coming. They would need supplies and a place to repair their wagons. In 1843 Jim decided to start such a place in Wyoming.

At first, Fort Bridger was only a trading post with a blacksmith shop and sheds for the animals. Later

The trickle of settlers to the West soon became a torrent. They brought prosperity to Fort Bridger— and doom to the Indians.

several log buildings were surrounded by a high picket fence to make it a fort.

It became an important way station for the pioneers traveling westward. Here they could trade for strong horses and oxen. They could hire guides or get information about the trails to Utah, California, or Oregon. Fort Bridger made the trip easier for thousands of pioneers.

But it was not to be a happy place for Jim. Three years after the fort was built, his wife, Cora, died.

Other tragedy soon followed. In March 1848, the snow was deep and the wind sharp and cold. Three men staggered into the fort, more dead than alive. Jim was surprised to see an old friend, Joe Meek.

Joe had married an Indian woman and had moved to Oregon.

"There's been Indian trouble up our way, Jim," he said. "Bad trouble. The Cayuse Indians went on the warpath. They burned the Whitman Mission. They killed Marcus and his wife." Joe Meek stopped. Jim Bridger sat in stunned silence.

At last Jim asked, "What happened to my Mary Ann, Joe?"

"I really don't know, Jim. They say she was carried off by the Indians."

Somehow Jim knew he would never see Mary Ann again. Later he learned that she was dead.

In time, Jim took another wife, a Ute Indian. When their child, Virginia, was born, the mother died.

While still at Fort Bridger, Jim married a third time. His last wife was named Little Faun. She was a lovely Shoshone princess.

Ever since Mary Ann's death, Jim had worried about the safety of his family. "Could you be happy among white people?" he asked Little Faun.

She smiled. "I can be happy anywhere."

"I'd like to get a farm in Missouri. There you can be safe, and Virginia can go to school."

So Jim moved his family to Missouri and tried to settle down.

The End of the Trail

Jim Bridger was not happy away from the mountains. Soon he returned to them. He spent many of his last years guiding wagon trains and the United States Army. The army was sent to survey the land and also to protect the settlers from Indian attacks.

Jim took good care of the groups he guided. He knew the Indians and how to go through their country.

While building Fort Phil Kearney, the army needed supplies from another fort, Fort Reno. Captain Burrows was sent to get them. Jim Bridger went along as guide and scout to the captain.

Along the trail that day, Jim found many buffalo skulls. On the bleached white bones were strange markings. They showed an arrow, a broken gun, and a woman with a zigzag line around her face.

These were signs of trouble up ahead—bad trouble.

When Captain Burrows gave orders to camp, Jim Bridger said, "I believe we'd better go on, captain."

"Go on!" the officer shouted. Then he looked at Jim's serious face. "Why do you say that, Jim?"

"There's going to be a fight on Crazy Woman Creek. The buffalo skulls tell all the Sioux to be there."

Captain Burrows looked at his 200 tired men. "You're sure, Jim?"

Jim Bridger nodded.

Captain Burrows still seemed doubtful. Then he roared, "Prepare to march! We will camp at Crazy Woman Creek tonight!"

Unhappy and grumbling, the tired men fell into line again.

At last they reached Crazy Woman Creek. Here they found 26 men who had been on their way to Fort Phil Kearney. Several hundred Sioux had attacked them from the surrounding hills. The arrival of Captain Burrows and his men sent the Indians fleeing and saved 26 lives.

In 1868 Jim Bridger left the army. He went to his

farm in Missouri. Here he lived with his daughter, Virginia.

Jim was old now. His health was beginning to fail, and he also found out that he was going blind.

But there were happy moments for Jim Bridger. The children who lived nearby discovered that Jim was a wonderful storyteller. They sat breathless as he told of the trappers and the Indians. They roared with laughter at his tall tales.

On July 17, 1881, when he was 77 years old, Jim Bridger died.

He had lived the life he loved—the life of a mountain man. He had discovered Great Salt Lake and had explored large areas of the West. He had been a great trapper and a brave army guide.

He is still remembered for his courage and his loyalty to his fellow trappers. Jim Bridger will always be known as a king of the mountain men.

"Buffler Comin'!"

The sun was climbing into the morning sky as a party of mountain men prepared to break camp. The trappers were crossing the broad plains on their way to a stream that had not been trapped for some time. They hoped to find plenty of beaver there. The mules stood ready for loading, and the saddled horses were hobbled a short distance away.

Suddenly a trapper rode furiously into camp. He had gone out earlier to scout the land. "Buffler!" he shouted. "Buffler comin' this way!"

All thought of breaking camp was now forgotten. The men had not tasted fresh buffalo meat for several weeks. The hunt was on!

Quickly they stripped themselves of any gear they would not need on the hunt. They tied scarves around their heads to keep the hair out of their eyes. Snatching up their loaded rifles, they dashed for their horses. Even as they ran, they fumbled bullets from their pouches and popped the lead balls into their mouths. There they would be handy for reloading the guns. Eyes shone with excitement as the trappers vaulted up on their horses. There was nothing to match a buffalo hunt for thrills. A man's first buffalo hunt was something he never forgot.

The trappers galloped out of camp, topped a rise, and saw the herd of buffalo in the distance. Thousands of the huge, shaggy-headed beasts stretched as far as the eye could see. They had not yet caught the scent of the half-dozen hunters and were moving slowly, grazing on buffalo grass. Dust rose from their plodding feet in a thick cloud.

The hunters reined their mounts to a sudden stop. One of the men leaped from his horse and plucked a stem of grass from the ground. He tossed it into the air and watched it drift with the wind. This told him which way the wind was coming from. The hunters rode against the wind so that the herd would not smell them and begin to stampede. To make a sure kill, the mountain men had to ride close to the buffalo's side and aim for the spine or lungs.

But the big beasts caught the man smell. The herd

began to run! The sound of thundering hooves was like the noise of an oncoming storm. The cloud of dust grew thicker. The hunters rode into it as they chased the buffalo. Soon they were surrounded by stampeding beasts. If a horse stumbled now on the rough ground, its rider might fall and be trampled to death under the pounding hooves. Yet the daring hunters guided their horses only with their knees! Their hands were free to use their guns.

Each man picked out a fat cow and edged alongside until his leg almost touched the buffalo. Then he took careful aim just behind the right shoulder. This was hard to do because of the dust in his eyes and the wild motion of his running horse. But a mountain man knew how to handle his gun. He fired. The buffalo stumbled and went down heavily.

Now the hunter had to reload while his horse raced at full speed. He quickly dumped powder down the muzzle and spat a bullet after it. He seated the bullet by slamming the gun butt down on his saddle. He poured more powder from the horn into the firing pan. It wasn't possible for him to measure carefully with his horse plunging under him. So he put in extra powder to make up for what would be spilled in the wild ride and went after his second cow.

By the end of the hunt, the mountain men were as tired as their horses. But there was more work to be done. The dead buffalo had to be butchered. That meant first getting the heavy animals—weighing almost as much as a ton—up on their bellies, with their legs spread out like braces to the sides. Sharp knives cut through tough hide along the spine. Then the skin was peeled down so the hunters could get at the meat underneath.

Veteran mountain men liked buffalo meat so much that they couldn't wait until they got back to camp for their first taste of the fresh kill. They cut out the liver and ate it raw, sometimes seasoning it with gunpowder. A greenhorn usually wasn't up to that on his first hunt, but he would take his first buffalo tail as a trophy.

What a feast there was in camp after a hunt! Each man usually built his own fire and did his own cooking. Some parts of the buffalo were boiled and others fried in buffalo fat. But most of the meat was roasted over the coals on the end of a ramrod or a green stick.

The men joked and laughed as the eating went on and on. They could stow away eight pounds at a sitting. Then they would fall over on their backs, rest a while, and come back to eat another eight pounds. Their hunting knives and hands were their only tableware. Their laps were their tables. By the time they were through, they were smeared with grease, blood, and juices. But they were wonderfully happy, and they laughed at the sight of one another's smeared faces. And none of them ever got sick from overeating!

Richard Glendinning

Trapping Tall Tales

Around the campfire at the end of day, in snug cabins during the long, cold winter, and at the rendezvous—wherever mountain men gathered—they swapped tall tales and manufactured stories. Their yarns got better in every telling! Here are a few.

THE AMAZING ALARM CLOCK

Jim Bridger was rated as one of the best at spinning tall tales. One of his most famous stories was about an "alarm clock" echo. He told the tale to show how big the wilderness was.

"When this ol' hoss turned in fer the night," Jim would say with a straight face, "all he had to do was yell, 'Time to git up!' Bless me if eight hours later that echo didn't come to rouse him out of his sleep!"

Richard Glendinning

YELLOWSTONE COUNTRY

With a twinkle in his eye, Jim told of an amazing lake he knew about. He said there was a boiling hot spring at the edge of the lake. When he caught a trout, all he had to do was to pull it through the spring to have the fish cooked by the time it came to him! When his friends hooted at that one, Jim went on to tell them about a swift river that was hot on the bottom from rushing so fast over the rocks!

Richard Glendinning

KIT CARSON
1809–1868

longed to join the wagon trains that
assembled in the little town of Franklin,
Missouri, for the dangerous journey
to Santa Fe. His opportunity came
when Captain Charles Bent hired the
undersized sixteen-year-old to tend the
livestock on his next caravan to the
Southwest. When the trip was over, Kit
joined a trapping expedition leaving
Taos, New Mexico, for the Rocky Mountains. From that time on his heart belonged to the great open spaces of the
western plains and mountains. Kit
trapped beaver, fought off grizzlies,
battled Indians, and led the great explorer John Charles Frémont westward.
When the price of beaver dropped and
the rip-roaring days of the mountain men
were over, Kit continued to live—and
finally died—in the Southwest he loved
so well.

Kit Carson

Pathfinder of the West

by Nardi Reeder Campion

Copyright © 1963 by Nardi Reeder Campion

"Merry Christmas, Mrs. Carson"

"Merry Christmas, Mrs. Carson," said Mr. Carson, bending over his wife's pillow. "Thank you for the gift you've brought us this Christmas Eve. December 24, 1809—that's a day to remember."

"Which is it?" asked his wife.

"A boy."

"*Another* boy?"

"Guess you'd like a girl, Becky, but the frontier needs men, and so do the Carsons."

"Let's call him Christopher," said Mrs. Carson. "Christopher Carson. Doesn't that sound important, Lindsay?"

"He looks too small for such a big name. Maybe we'd better shorten it to Kit."

Christopher Carson never grew to fit his long name. His small size always made him very unhappy. Once, when Kit was a small boy, he overheard his mother and father talking about him. "Lindsay," said his mother, "I wish you wouldn't let little Kit chop down trees. Let the big boys do it. He's too small for that dangerous work."

"Chopping isn't so dangerous, Becky, if you watch out. Kit's the runt of the litter, all right. But out of ten children, one puny one isn't bad."

Kit felt as though his father had hit him in the face. "The runt of the litter?" He didn't weigh much, and his legs were short. But was he a runt? Kit looked into the bit of broken glass the Carsons used for a mirror. He saw a blue-eyed, sandy-haired boy. He saw a face tanned and freckled by the sun. "I may be small," he thought, "but I'm strong. I'll show them."

"Lindsay Carson," Kit's mother was saying, "I don't think you know what the word *danger* means. If you had known, we wouldn't have left Kentucky. Here in Missouri wild animals and Indians are everywhere."

"My folks came over from Scotland 50 years ago, Becky. They weren't looking for safety and comfort. They were pioneers. And that's what we are, Becky, *pioneers*. And danger is our middle name."

Life on the frontier was rugged. The Carson children did not go to school. But they learned the ways of the woods from their father. Kit could not read or write, yet he knew the names of all the trees and how each was used. He knew the habits of the wild animals. He could build clever traps to catch them.

Kit worked hard to make up for his size. He used his eyes and ears. He noticed all sounds and animal tracks. He taught himself to "freeze." He could hold

so still that animals and Indians did not know he was nearby.

Kit was happy in the forest, except for one thing. He did not have a gun. He had to hunt with a bow and arrow. His eyes were keen. He could hit a squirrel on the run with an arrow. But he wanted a gun.

On his birthday, Kit begged his father, "Now that I'm nine, can't I have a gun? I want a flintlock rifle, just like yours."

His father shook his head.

"Why not? I can hit a nail head at 20 feet with your gun."

"Oh, you're a good shot, Kit. I'm proud of that. But we are too poor. We can't buy another gun. Maybe if we can trap a lot of beaver next spring. . . . Now come along and help me burn trees in the field we're clearing for a corn patch."

Kit's eyes filled with tears. Nobody knew how much he wanted a gun.

All that day Kit and his brother Big Mose worked with their father. They chopped trees and cleared land in the cold autumn sunshine. As night fell, they made a roaring brush fire. Lindsay Carson would not stop. He picked up his axe and attacked another tree. Suddenly Kit heard a crack and then a scream. He turned and saw a big limb crash down on his father. Lindsay Carson fell to the ground.

93

Kit helped his father and brother clear the land for planting (painting by George Harvey).

Kit and his brother ran to him. They could not move the heavy oak branch. "What will we do?" yelled Big Mose. Little Kit bent double and crawled underneath the branch. When he reached his father, he found that he was dead.

That night Kit was sitting by the fire with his head in his hands. Death was common enough on the frontier. But this was different. Kit began to sob. Then he felt a hand on his shoulder. He looked up. His mother was standing beside him. In her hand was his father's flintlock rifle. She held it out to Kit.

"This is your gun now, Christopher," she said. "You're no longer a boy. Today you became a man."

Oh, to Be a Mountain Man!

"I don't want to be a saddle maker, mother," said Kit Carson. "I'm going to be a hunter and trapper. I want to live in the forest and be free."

"No, Christopher. You are going to be an apprentice and learn a trade. Hurry now, Mr. Workman is expecting you."

Mr. David Workman's gloomy saddle shop smelled of dust and leather. Its stale air made Kit cough. Mr. Workman scowled. "Just sign the papers please, ma'am," he said.

"What do the papers say?" asked Mrs. Carson.

"That yonder boy is bound out to David Workman, saddler, of Franklin, Missouri, for seven years."

"Seven years!" thought Kit. "I won't last seven weeks in this dust bin. I need air."

Mrs. Carson and Kit each drew an "X" on the paper. Neither one could read or write.

"Good-bye, son," said Mrs. Carson. "Work hard." There were tears in her eyes.

"Do my best, ma," said Kit. He tried hard to swallow the lump in his throat.

Mr. Workman was a kind man, but he expected a lot of Kit. Kit hated being shut up in the shop, making saddles. Outside he could see the wagon trains getting ready to go West. How he longed to join them!

The mountain men came into the shop to get their saddles and harnesses fixed. Kit listened eagerly to their tales of danger, hunger, blood, and sweat. His head hummed with dreams of adventure.

"Boy!" yelled Mr. Workman. "Watch what you're doing! That gun cover is beginning to look like a pillowcase."

Kit tried to pay attention. Even as a boy, he wanted to do things well. But Kit Carson's heart was always outdoors with the mountain men. One day he could stand it no longer. After Mr. Workman went to lunch, Kit left the shop. He stopped the first mountain man he saw.

"Mister, don't you need a helper? I'll do anything you ask—anything. Please take me West with you."

The frontiersman looked down at the eager blond boy. Then he laughed. "What do you think we're running? A nursery?"

Kit gasped, "But mister, I'm fifteen."

"You look about ten. So you want to go West? I'll give you some advice. Grow up!"

Kit walked slowly back to the shop. His head hung down. He was miserable. "Grow up?" he thought. "I'm as big as I'll ever be."

It wasn't until a year later that Kit got his chance. One day, when Mr. Workman was out, a stranger came into the shop. He was dressed in buckskins trimmed with fringe and beads.

"Captain Charles Bent?" asked Kit.

"How'd you know my name?" said the man.

"Everybody knows you, Captain Bent. I guess you're the most famous trader there is."

Captain Bent looked pleased.

"I've been watching you get your wagon train ready, sir. I've counted 28 wagons."

"Right. We start rolling toward Santa Fe in the morning."

"Captain Bent!" Kit's heart was pounding so fast he could scarcely talk. "You *must* need an extra hand. Do you, sir? Do you?"

"What about your job here?" Captain Bent asked.

"Oh, Mr. Workman wouldn't miss me. He doesn't think I'm worth anything." This was not quite true, but Kit was desperate.

Charles Bent looked the boy over carefully. There was something about him. "Can you ride?" he asked.

"Yes, sir. Rode before I walked."

"Are you afraid of Indians?"

"No, sir."

"You got a gun?"

"Got my pa's. And I can shoot it."

Bent rubbed his beard. "I could use another cavvy boy to help on this trip. The cavvy boys take care of the extra horses, mules, and cattle."

"I can do that," said Kit. "I know I can." His eyes were shining.

"I like the look of you, lad. Come 'round to my wagon tonight. I'll get you a mule to ride. We hit the trail at sunup." Bent started toward the door. Then he called back. "Oh, yes. One more thing. I pay cavvy boys a dollar a day."

Captain Bent strode out into the sunlight. Kit sat down and shook his head. A dollar a day! Why, he would have *paid* to go with Captain Bent. That is, he would have, if he had had any money. Captain Charles Bent was a great man. And he had not even mentioned Kit's small size!

One Cent Reward

Kit pulled his blanket around him. He was tired, but he could not sleep. The ground was hard. He ached all over. He sat up and rubbed his back. In the moonlight the white-topped wagons looked like ghostly sailboats.

Yeee-o-o-o-w. A howl came out of the night. Kit shivered. Wolves! He moved closer to the campfire.

"It's only sixteen miles back to Franklin," said a voice. Kit whirled around. Behind him stood Captain Bent. "It's not too late to turn back, lad."

Fear gripped Kit. "Ain't I doing the job right, captain?"

Bent smiled. "You're doing fine, lad. I watched you. You have spunk."

Captain Bent's words helped Kit. He needed encouragement.

The trip to Santa Fe was long and hard. Soon the food ran low. They had nothing to eat except coffee and salt pork.

Captain Bent sent for Kit. "Lad," he said, "you're a fast rider. Gallop ahead and look for food. We're close to starvation."

Kit was proud to be given such a job. But at the end of the day he returned, discouraged. Across his saddle hung a dead wolf.

"Captain," said Kit, "I'm a failure. All I could find was a pack of wolves."

"Wolves!" cried Bent. "Great! How far away?"

"Just beyond the river. But, captain, what good are wolves?"

"Oh, you've a lot to learn, lad. Wolves mean buffalo. The wolf pack follows the buffalo herd. They want meat as much as we do. Let's go!"

Captain Bent was a skilled hunter. That night Kit ate roasted buffalo under the stars. Kit ate a lot of buffalo in his lifetime. But it never tasted as good as it did that first night.

At last Captain Bent's wagon train rolled into Santa Fe. Kit liked the Mexican town with its narrow

Cheers and shouts filled the air when a caravan at last sighted the beautiful city of Santa Fe.

streets and pretty girls. Captain Bent was returning to Missouri. But Kit had no desire to go back right away. He called on Captain Bent to say good-bye.

"Sit down, lad," said Captain Bent. "This Missouri paper just came in by stagecoach. I want to read you one of the ads."

> Notice: Christopher Carson, a boy about 16, small for his age, but thickset and light haired, ran away about September 1st. He was bound to me to learn the saddler's trade. All persons are warned not to hide this runaway. One cent reward will be given to anyone who brings him back.
>
> David Workman
> Franklin, Missouri
> October 6, 1826

Kit turned pale.

Captain Bent shook his head sadly. "I'll have to send you back, lad."

Kit doubled up his fists. He felt like crying. Then he looked closely at Captain Bent. The captain's blue eyes were twinkling. The older man threw back his head and laughed.

"*One cent reward!* Ho! Ho! Ho! Pretty cheap price!"

Kit began to laugh too. "I told you, sir, Mr. Workman didn't think I was worth much."

"Well," said the captain, "I could tell Mr. Workman some news. Kit Carson may be young, and he may be small. But he's worth a whole lot. He's the best trail rider I've seen in years."

Kit grinned. He felt eight feet tall.

Attack!

After Captain Bent left, Kit did not know where to turn. He couldn't find a job in Santa Fe. A few scouts from Captain Bent's caravan were going to nearby Taos, and Kit joined them. Taos was headquarters for the mountain men. But it was no place for an undersized boy to find work. Soon all of Kit's money was gone.

Then he ran into a piece of good luck. At Ewing Young's Trading Post he saw a man he knew. It was Old Kincade, who had lived near the Carsons in Missouri.

"Well, bless my soul, boy," said Old Kincade, "you got no place to live? Just come right out to my hut."

Old Kincade was poor and sick, but he had been a great hunter. He taught Kit many things. "Now, son," he would say, "you got a good memory. I know that by the easy way you pick up Spanish and Indian talk.

"We got no maps out here, just memory. So you put your memory to work. Never turn a bend in a hurry. Look back and learn the lay of the land. Never leave a river in a hurry. They're all different. Learn how it tastes and looks and runs. Then you'll know it when you see it again. Keep looking and learning all the time, Kit."

When spring came, poor Kincade died. Kit hit the trail again. He hiked 80 miles back to Santa Fe. He lived on rabbits and prairie dogs. But he still could not find a job. He walked the 80 miles back to Taos. He went straight to Young's Trading Post.

"Captain Young," he pleaded, "please let me work for you."

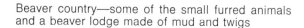

Beaver country—some of the small furred animals and a beaver lodge made of mud and twigs

Young looked Kit over. "You're too small," he said bluntly.

Kit groaned. "That's what they told me in Santa Fe."

Young looked puzzled. "How did you get here from Santa Fe?"

"Walked."

"WALKED? How long did it take?"

"Three days."

"What did you eat?"

"Anything I shot."

There was a long silence. Then Ewing Young spoke again. "You're hired. You're small, but you're tough. I'm heading north with 40 men to trap beaver. We can use you."

"Mr. Young, why is everyone crazy over beaver?" asked Kit.

"All the men back East and in England, too, are wearing high hats made of beaver. It's the style. A trapper can get rich on beaver."

That year Kit learned a lot about trapping beaver. The best time to catch beaver is when the weather is cold. Then their coats are thickest. But you have to catch them before the streams they live in are frozen.

Kit learned to spot signs of beaver. Beaver use logs to build houses and dam up streams. A bit of torn bark or a chewed tree told Kit beaver were nearby. He learned that beaver can smell a man a mile away.

Only water washes away the smell of man. Kit waded into swift, icy rivers to set the traps. The traps were heavy to carry. They were built to hold a 50-pound beaver when he was fighting mad.

Captain Young taught Kit how to skin a beaver and how to stretch the skin on sticks to dry. He showed him how to roast the body and eat it.

The trappers were always in danger from the Indians. One day Young's men were working along the Salt River. Suddenly Ewing Young held up his hand, warning the men to be quiet. They knew what he meant. *Indians!*

"Grab your guns," whispered Young. "Head back to camp. Hide under blankets, packs, anything. Hide!"

Back they ran. Kit crawled under his blanket. He held on to his father's gun. His heart beat fast. This seemed an odd way to fight Indians.

Kit peeped out. The ridge above was covered with Indians. Young and his 40 men were clearly outnumbered.

"We'll all be scalped," thought Kit.

"Hold your fire," whispered Young. "They'll think we've gone."

Kit listened to the Indians coming nearer and nearer. He wished Captain Young would let them shoot. Now the Indians were right in the camp. Then Young shouted, "FIRE!"

Indians dropped on every side. The others turned and ran. Some of Young's men chased them over the ridge.

When the attack was over, fifteen Indians lay dead. Kit felt sick. He had never killed a man before. Young put his arm around the boy.

"Bad, isn't it?" he said. "But with a fighting Indian, it's him or you every time. Remember that, Kit."

Little Chief of the Cheyennes

Ewing Young liked Kit Carson. He took Kit on a trip to California. It was almost the end for both of them. Crossing the desert, the entire party nearly died of thirst. They were also attacked by Indians. Kit Carson was going to a rough school.

On his return, Kit went trapping again in the Rockies. He went with famous mountain men like Jim Bridger. Then he heard that Captain Bent was looking for men. Kit rode along the Arkansas River until he found him.

Captain Bent was glad to see his young friend. "How old are you now, lad?"

"Twenty-two," said Kit. Then he added sadly, "Haven't grown taller, just older."

"Is that your own horse?"

"Yes, sir, I bought him with the money I made

trapping beaver. His name is Squaw Man." Kit rubbed his horse's neck proudly.

"How would you like to work for me, lad?" asked Bent. "The Indians keep raiding my trading post, so I'm building a fort. I need a good man to take charge of the log-cutting crew."

Kit beamed. "I'd like that fine."

Kit lost no time setting up the logging camp. Captain Bent gave him a crew of strong men. The work went well.

One cold winter night two friendly Cheyenne Indians visited the camp. Their names were Little Turtle and Black Whiteman. When they tied up their ponies, they were surprised no one was guarding the horses. But they said nothing.

In the morning, only the two Indian ponies were left. All the other horses were gone.

During the night, 60 Crow Indians had crept into the camp. They stole all the horses. They did not want Indian ponies.

Kit Carson did not lose his temper easily. But now he was hopping mad. "Grab your blanket rolls, men," he yelled. "We're going after them."

The men thought Kit was out of his mind. "The Crows have a 20-mile lead," they said. "How can we catch them? We have to travel on foot."

Kit knew he ought to go back to the trading post

The fort that the Bents built on the Arkansas River became Kit Carson's second home. His first was the great open spaces of the West.

for help. But he was ashamed to face Captain Bent. He was angry at himself for leaving the horses unguarded.

"We're going," he said stubbornly. "The Crows won't be looking for us. They left a clear trail. We can follow it easily. We *must* get back our horses." Squaw Man was the only thing Kit owned, other than his father's gun.

Only a real leader could get men to go on such a hopeless chase. But the men followed Kit Carson. Black Whiteman and Little Turtle rode along beside them, laughing. They thought Kit was crazy.

For two full days, Kit and his men trudged northward. When they reached the Rockies, they ran into snow. The wind stung their faces. They plodded on without speaking. They did not want Indians to hear them.

Suddenly Kit pointed ahead. Smoke rose from a clump of pines. They had found what they were looking for.

"You two ride ahead and hide," Kit said to Little Turtle and Black Whiteman. "When we attack, you can get the horses."

The two friendly Indians nodded. By now, even they wanted to do what Kit Carson said.

Kit and his men crept quietly toward the Crow's camp.

Suddenly a dog jumped out of the bushes. In a flash, the Crows came charging through the pine trees. They waved bows and arrows and scalping knives.

Kit remembered something he learned from Ewing Young. "Hide!" he yelled. "Hold your fire. Don't shoot till I tell you!"

Kit and his men ducked behind trees and bushes. The Indians thundered toward them. When Kit could almost touch their leader, he shouted, "FIRE!"

All the guns banged at once. Three Indians fell. The rest dashed toward the pines. Kit and his men ran after them.

The Crows raced after the horses. But the horses were gone! In a panic, the Crows fled. They thought a large force was after them.

Kit's men threw themselves on the ground. They were panting and sweating. Little Turtle and Black Whiteman rode up with the horses. The men cheered. They shook Kit's hand. Kit ran to get Squaw Man. Happily he rubbed his horse's nose.

The men rode the horses back to Bent's Trading Post. Little Turtle and Black Whiteman went back to the Cheyennes. They told everyone how Kit Carson had outfought the fierce Crows. Yellow Wolf, chief of the Cheyennes, listened. Then he rode his pony to Bent's Fort.

"I wish to see the small white leader who chased the Crows," he told Bent.

Bent sent for Kit. All the other men gathered around and watched.

"Small white man," commanded Yellow Wolf, "kneel down."

Kit was puzzled, but he did as he was told. The chief raised his hand above Kit's head.

"My son," he said, "you have a brave heart. You went after your horses on foot and got them back. With few men, you beat many Crows. From this day, among my people, your name will be *Vih'hui-nis*, Little Chief of the Cheyennes."

Preparing for a Buffalo

Saved by a Nose

Kit Carson was becoming famous throughout the Rockies. Now he no longer worked for others. He arranged his own expeditions. He was the leader. Many men wanted to sign up with him, but Kit would take only a few good men. No one could judge a trapper better than Kit Carson.

One summer Kit and his party trapped in the Medicine Bow Mountains. They had good luck. But as winter came on, their food grew scarce. Kit started searching for game.

One afternoon he galloped into camp. "At last I found something," he said. "I saw signs of elk. I'm going to track the elk on foot."

Tom Cotton, one of the trappers, brought Kit's flintlock. "Want me to go with you?"

"No. It's better alone. Tonight we eat elk, Tom, or I'm a monkey's uncle."

Kit started off into the woods. "Don't let Uncle Grizzly get you," called Tom.

Kit's moccasins padded silently along the trail. He sniffed the air like a bloodhound. He knew Tom was not joking. This was grizzly bear country. No Indian would venture into grizzly country alone.

The grizzly bear is the most dangerous animal in the Rocky Mountains. He is also the strongest. A full-grown

111

This party of trappers is about to leave camp in search of game (painting by Alfred Jacob Miller).

grizzly weighs more than 1,000 pounds and is 7 feet tall. His front paws, which he uses like hands, are a foot wide. He is clever, fearless, and fierce.

But Kit Carson was not thinking about danger. His men needed food. He meant to get it for them, no matter what the risk. Like all real leaders, Kit Carson thought of his men first.

Kit followed the elk tracks for several miles. At last he found a herd of fat elk grazing on a hillside. Carefully, Kit crept into a clump of pines. Now the elk were in front of him. He raised his gun and fired. One buck staggered and fell; the others vanished.

Kit ran forward. Suddenly, he heard a roar behind him. He whirled around. Two huge grizzly bears were charging toward him.

Kit thought fast. His gun was empty. He could not reload now. He could see the bears' teeth flashing. He knew their sharp claws were ready to tear him to bits.

Kit had only one chance. He dropped his precious gun and ran. He ran as he had never run before.

In a short race a grizzly can outrun a race horse. But Kit was trying to outrun death. He streaked for cover. If only he could reach the trees! Kit pounded over the ground. The bears were hot behind him. He grabbed a branch and swung himself into a tree. One bear stabbed at Kit with his big paw. It ripped off a moccasin. Kit scrambled up higher.

Bears climb trees, and Kit knew it. He pulled out his hunting knife. He hacked off a short, thick branch to use as a club. "I don't think a bear can climb this small a tree," thought Kit, "but I can. Maybe it's lucky to be little."

The male grizzly was furious. He fumed and raged and foamed at the mouth. He backed away and charged the tree. His thousand-pound body shook it like a hurricane. Kit hugged the tree. He held on.

Again and again the big bear beat against the tree. When it would not break, he began to bellow and snort. He jerked small trees from the ground. He clawed at the roots of Kit's tree. Then he tried to climb up it. The trunk bent over.

"This is the end," thought Kit.

The bear's paw raked Kit's drawn-up legs. Kit clutched the club he had cut. CRASH! He banged it down on the bear's nose. Crash! Crash! Crash! Kit clubbed the bear again and again.

The grizzly gave a scream of pain. He fell to the ground. He rolled over and over.

Kit was so weak he could hardly hang on to the tree. He leaned his head against the trunk and waited to see what would happen.

The bear picked himself up. He shook himself and joined his mate, who was eating the dead elk.

Kit clung to the tree. He thought, "I said we'd eat

elk, or I'm a monkey's uncle. Guess I look like a monkey's uncle. I feel like one too."

The moon rose, and the wind moaned in the trees. Kit still did not move from his branch. It was midnight before he dared drop to the ground.

He picked up his gun and ran for camp. His men were huddled around the fire, waiting. They were afraid something had happened to him. They were right— something had. For the rest of his life, Kit Carson called his escape from the grizzly bears "my worst difficult experience."

Singing Grass

The trapping season ended after the beavers shed their winter coats. Then the trappers enjoyed themselves. In the summer of 1835, the trappers, traders, and Indians held a great get-together in the Green River Valley. It was called a rendezvous. These get-togethers were the biggest event in a mountain man's year.

Their camp-out lasted as long as the hot weather. They enjoyed wrestling, horse racing, shooting, and dancing. There were lots of contests with the friendly Indians.

Kit Carson and his friend, big Jim Bridger, hurried to the Green River Valley to join the fun. They liked to visit the Arapaho Indians who were camped nearby.

The Arapahos were the happiest of all tribes. They hated fighting and killing. They loved music, dancing, and laughter, and they sang beautifully.

Every evening the Arapahos danced in a meadow by the river. One evening, Kit and Jim arrived at sunset. The dancing was going full tilt.

"Psst," whispered Jim, poking Kit, "I smell trouble." He pointed to a man watching the dancers. Kit recognized the giant French-Canadian called Shunar.

Shunar was a well-known bully. Wherever he went, he started a fight. He liked to find smaller men and beat them to a pulp. No one dared stand up to Shunar the Bully.

Shunar had been drinking firewater and was unsteady on his feet. His eyes were on one of the dancing girls. Kit followed the bully's gaze. The young Indian was beautiful. She wore a white buckskin dress trimmed with colored beads. Her smooth black hair shone in the firelight. Her skin was golden brown.

"You can't speak to an Arapaho girl without her father's permission," said Jim. "Look at that Shunar. He's going after her."

Shunar pushed through the dancers. He knocked young braves right and left. He grabbed the beautiful Indian maiden and tried to kiss her. Quick as a flash, she slapped his face. She tore herself loose and raced lightly into the woods.

BOOM! BOOM! BOOM! Indian drums suddenly began beating war chants. Shunar stood in the middle of the ring, glaring. He looked like an angry ape.

"White man touch Waa-nibe," thundered the chief. "Indian kill him." The braves began to close in on Shunar.

"WAIT!" Kit Carson held up his hand. He stalked up to the giant Shunar. "Lay your hands on another woman, Shunar, and I'll rip you to pieces."

Like all bullies, Shunar wanted to scare people. But he could see Kit was not afraid. Shunar ran. He grabbed his gun and jumped on his horse. Kit jumped on Squaw Man. He clutched his father's flintlock.

The two men charged at each other. ZOW! They both fired. Shunar's bullet ripped through Kit's hair. Kit's bullet hit Shunar's heart. The bully tumbled over, dead.

That night, Kit could not sleep. But he wasn't worrying about Shunar's death. Shunar had killed many good men. Like a mad dog, he had to be put away. Kit could not sleep because he was thinking about the Indian girl. "Waa-nibe means Singing Grass," Kit thought. "She is as lovely as her name."

Next day Waa-nibe's father sent for Kit. He wanted to thank him. Kit gazed at Waa-nibe. She gave him a shy smile. Kit's heart melted.

Not long afterward, Kit Carson and Waa-nibe were married. The Indian wedding took place in her father's

Kit Carson's marriage to Waa-nibe may have been similar to this wedding between a trapper and an Indian girl (painting by Alfred Jacob Miller).

lodge. The chief spread his blanket over the shoulders of Waa-nibe and the "Little Chief of the Cheyennes." This meant Kit and Waa-nibe were now man and wife.

The Pathfinder's Pathfinder

From his young Indian bride Kit learned many things. He began to understand the way Indians thought.

A baby girl was born to the young couple. Kit was happy because she looked like her beautiful mother. "We will call her Adaline," he said.

Waa-nibe nodded. Good Indian wives always agreed with their husbands.

Kit now had a new reason to go trapping. "You and Adaline will stay at Bent's Fort," he said. "I'll trap the Blackfoot country."

"But the Blackfoot land is full of danger," said Waa-nibe.

"It's also full of beaver," said Kit. "I'll make a lot of money. Then we'll settle in Taos. We'll live quietly and raise a family."

Waa-nibe knew this was a dream. Kit Carson could never settle down. To tame him would be like putting an eagle in a birdcage.

Kit took 40 of his "Carson men" with him on this trapping expedition. They were successful wherever they went.

One day a messenger came riding after Kit. He had some terrible news. Waa-nibe was ill. She had prairie fever. To reach her, Kit rode Squaw Man 180 miles in 2 days. Kit rushed to Waa-nibe's bedside. His wife died in his arms.

Kit was heartbroken. Captain Bent tried to comfort him. "Death is part of life, lad," he said.

"How will I take care of Adaline?" moaned Kit.

"The frontier is no place for a motherless girl," said Bent. "Have you relatives who could care for her?"

"I have a sister in St. Louis," Kit muttered.

"You should take Adaline to her," said Captain Bent.

Kit did as the captain suggested. He hated to say good-bye to his daughter. But his sister loved the child at first sight. That made it easier.

On the riverboat returning from St. Louis, Kit made a new friend. This friendship became important. It helped shape the history of the American West.

Kit was standing on deck when a stranger spoke to him. "I'm Charles Frémont," he said. "They tell me you're the famous Indian scout, Kit Carson."

"Not very famous," mumbled Kit.

"I'm going West to map the Oregon country for the government," Frémont said. "I'm going to need help. Are you interested?"

"I can't read or write," said Kit. "I don't own a compass or a watch. What help would I be?"

Kit Carson (standing) became a guide for the famous explorer of the West, John Charles Frémont (seated).

Frémont laughed. "I hear your mind *is* a map. They say you know every stream, canyon, and mountain in the West. I want you to act as my guide. I'll pay you 100 dollars a month."

Thus began the famous friendship. With Kit as his guide, Frémont explored and mapped the Oregon Trail. Kit saved Frémont's life several times.

When his job was done, Kit hurried back to Taos to see Captain Bent's sister-in-law, Josefa Jaramillo. He had fallen in love with her, although she was 15 and he was 35. But young Josefa was both wise and beautiful. She and Kit were married in 1843.

Kit and Josefa had several children. Still, Kit never really settled down. He took Frémont on two more expeditions. They brought back valuable maps and information about the West. They even found a way over the Sierra Nevada Mountains. It is still called Carson Pass.

John Charles Frémont became a famous man. He was called "The Pathfinder." But those who knew said that Kit Carson was "The Pathfinder's Pathfinder."

Adios

Kit Carson is remembered for his reckless bravery. Yet in his later years, his work among the Indians was just as remarkable.

In 1853 Kit was made Indian agent in Taos. He held his job for seven years. He did great work helping the whites to understand the Indians. "There were few bad Indians before the white man took away their means of gaining a living," Kit told the government. "The Indian is starving. It is your responsibility to feed him."

When the Civil War began, Kit became a soldier. He was a colonel in the New Mexico Volunteers. He fought bravely, but he hated war. He was glad when the war ended.

Now Kit could go back to his work with the Indians. He worked hard for the Indian Treaty Commission. General John Pope said: "Carson is the best man in the country to control these Indians. He is personally known and liked by every Indian of the bands likely to make trouble."

But Kit's time was running out. His health was poor. He was hurt badly when he fell from a wild horse. When Josefa died, Kit's spirit was broken.

On May 23, 1868, after Josefa's death, Kit and a doctor friend sat talking. "Kit," the doctor teased, "they sure tamed the 'Pathfinder of the West.' You used to be as wild as a mustang."

Kit leaned back and closed his eyes. "Doc, it wasn't me that changed. It was my world. The mountains are covered with roads now. Even that railroad is coming out here. My world's gone, Doc."

The two men fell silent. The sun set. Kit lit up his pipe.

"Didn't I tell you not to smoke?" asked the doctor.

"Indeed you did." A twinkle came into Kit's tired eyes. "You told me to eat mush too. But I just finished a big steak and a cup of black coffee." Kit blew a cloud of smoke. "I'm not afraid of doctors or death— just grizzly bears!"

Doc laughed, but he was worried. No matter what he did, Kit's health grew worse. Everyone knew the end must be near.

Suddenly, Kit began coughing. He doubled up with pain. Doc bent over him, but there was nothing he could do. "I'm gone," Kit whispered. "*Adios, compadre.* Good-bye, my friend."

With those words, Kit Carson died. And with him died the wild, uncharted West.

> *The rails were made,*
> *The wars were won,*
> *Ole Kit Carson,*
> *His job was done.*

Equipped for Action!

Mountain men learned from their Indian friends to wear buckskin clothing, elk-hide moccasins, and fur hats to protect themselves against cold and stormy weather.

But their treasured equipment came from the East. A trapper's rifle was his friend, protector, and trusted right hand in the wilderness. Shown on the opposite page is the Hawken rifle which belonged to famous mountain man Jim Bridger.

Only second in importance were their traps. Those shown are of various sizes, used to hunt otter, beaver, and bears. The wooden stretcher at the far right was used to dry these furs.

Although some mountain men learned to ride with simple gear as the Indians did, a well-made saddle was a valued possession. This one is a special kind used by a trapper riding at the head of a mule team.

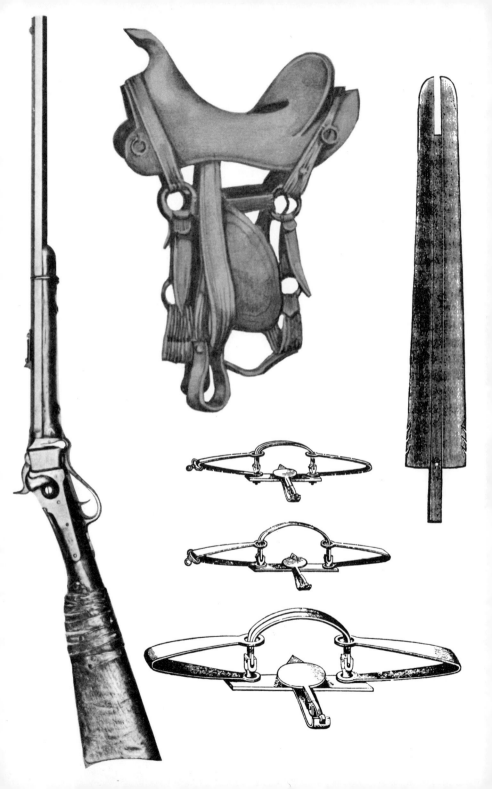

More Tales—Tall and Otherwise

MOUNT HOOD HIJINKS

Good-natured Joe Meek was another great storyteller. A greenhorn once asked him if he'd seen many changes come to the West. Joe had a quick answer. "I shorely have," he said. "Why, when I first come out here, Mount Hood, which is the highest mountain in the Oregon Country, warn't nothin' but a hole in the ground!"

Richard Glendinning

FELLED BY A MOUNTAIN

There were dozens of "glass mountain" stories! This was one trapper's version:

"Once I was up on the Yellowstone. I was walking along, looking for beaver signs and *bam*! I was flat on my back. Thought for sure I had been shot, but there wasn't no sound of a gun. So I started off again and *bam!* There I was on my back again with my nose bleeding. This time I got up with my hands out in front of me. And I felt it. And you know what it was?"

"It's your lie. You tell it."

"A mountain of pure glass! It was so clear that I walked right into it!"

Wyatt Blassingame

SUDDEN DEATH

Jim Bridger told about the time he was trying to escape on horseback from six Indians. He managed to pick off five of them, but the sixth followed close at his heels.

"We wus nearin' the edge of a deep and wide canyon," said Bridger. "No horse could leap over that awful chasm and a fall to the bottom meant sartin death. I turned my horse suddenly and the Injun was upon me. We both fired at once an' both horses wus killed. We now fought hand-to-hand with butcher knives. He was a powerful Injun—tallest I ever see. One moment I had the best of it and the next the odds wus agin me. Finally—"

Here Bridger paused as if to get breath.

"How did it end?" asked one of his listeners.

"*The Injun killed me,*" he replied slowly with a wink.

Captain J. Lee Humfreville

A SALTY STORY

Not all of the stories were made up. Jim Bridger once told one that no one believed for a while. But it was true. He said he had floated down the swift Bear River in a round boat made of buffalo hides stretched on a frame of willow boughs. It was a wild ride through steep-walled canyons. He came at last to a huge body of water. Jim leaned over for a drink. The water was so salty he spit it out. Jim thought he had come to the Pacific Ocean. Other trappers howled with laughter at what they took to be another of Jim's tall tales.

But the truth was that Bridger had discovered the Great Salt Lake in what is now Utah!

Richard Glendinning

FROZEN FOOD

On bitter nights about the fire, Jim Bridger liked to tell about an amazing snowstorm one winter in the valley of that very same lake. It went on for seventy days without stopping until the valley was covered with seventy feet of snow. The huge herds of buffalo that roamed the area were trapped in the snowstorm and died, but their carcasses, frozen stiff in the bitter cold, were well preserved.

"When things warmed up a bit," Jim told his listeners, "all I had to do was to push those buffalo into the Salt Lake, and I had enough pickled meat to feed myself and the whole Ute nation for years!"

A Greenhorn's Dictionary

beaver "medicine": a mixture of beaver glands and herbs used as bait to attract beaver to traps

boss: the hump on the back of a buffalo's neck

breechclout: a cloth worn by the trappers in warm weather instead of trousers

buckskins: leather clothing made from the skins of elk and deer

bullboat: a round boat made of fresh buffalo hides which were sewn together and stretched over a framework of willow limbs

cache: a hole in the ground in which mountain men hid furs

cavvy: a herd of extra animals following a wagon train

cold camp: a camp which had no campfire, where trappers slept without fear of attack

geyser: a spring which shoots streams of steam and boiling water into the air from time to time

greenhorn: a man who was new to the West, especially one who was not hardened to frontier life

hobble: to fasten the legs of an animal together so that it will not stray; also a strip of leather used to fasten the animal's legs

jerky: meat which has been cut into long strips and dried in the sun

keelboat: a shallow riverboat used by traders to carry furs and supplies

leggings: coverings for the legs, usually made of cloth or leather

pelt: the skin of a fur-bearing animal

possibles sack: a leather bag of things a mountain man might need in the wilderness

prairie schooners: the covered wagons which carried traders and settlers westward

ramrod: a rod used for ramming a charge into the muzzle of a firearm

rendezvous: the yearly meeting at which trappers, traders, and Indians swapped furs for goods

tethers: lines used for hitching or leading animals

traplines: a line or series of traps set by mountain men

BUFFALO BILL
1846–1917

was born when the glory days of the fur
trade were just about over. The West was
far from won, however. The story of
Buffalo Bill's life mirrors all the great
changes and movements that linked the
mountain men's rugged West with the
staid and settled East. Bill Cody faced
danger daily on the great wagon trains
that brought supplies to the West. He
outrode robbers on the Pony Express. He
fought as a scout for the Union army in
the Civil War. After the war, he worked
as a buffalo hunter for the railroads
stretching westward. Soon the buffalo
had almost all been wiped out by greedy
hunters who crowded the plains, and
the Indians were confined to reserva-
tions. Bill took to the road with his
Wild West Show. Americans and Euro-
peans alike thrilled to sharpshooters,
Indians, and a real live buffalo hunt. But
the way of life Bill glorified had already
vanished.

Buffalo Bill

Wild West Showman

by Mary R. Davidson

Copyright © 1962 by Mary R. Davidson

Growing Up in Kansas

Young Bill Cody lived in a small town near Fort Leavenworth, Kansas. But he had not always lived there. He had been born in Iowa in 1846. Then his father had taken his wife and Billy and the girls West.

Here the great freight wagon trains started out. They took food and guns to the forts and the settlers on the frontier. Each wagon was pulled by twelve strong oxen.

For a while all went well with the Cody family in Kansas. Then something dreadful happened.

Billy and his father were out riding. As they came to a store, they heard a crowd of rough men shouting. These men were talking about whether there should be slaves in the new state of Kansas. One of these men was drunk. He ran up to Mr. Cody. He pulled him off his horse.

"Here's a man who's against us," he said. He yelled at Mr. Cody, "Do you believe in bringing slaves to Kansas?"

Mr. Cody answered, "I do not. I do not believe that men ought to buy and sell other men."

Another drunken man leaped at Mr. Cody. He stabbed him in the back. Mr. Cody was bleeding badly. Billy and a friend borrowed a wagon and got him home. As they were leaving, a man shouted, "We'll get you yet."

Mrs. Cody nursed her husband until he was somewhat better. But Billy felt his father was not safe. He was afraid the men would come after him. Billy and his mother dressed Mr. Cody in women's clothes. Then they hid him in the cornfield. They made a comfortable bed for him there and took him food day and night.

Mr. Cody was soon moved to a friend's home, 20 miles away. But the mob learned of his new hiding place. Billy raced there on Prince to warn his father.

Again Mr. Cody came home. But he did not live for long.

When his father died, Billy was the only man in the family. He had to support his mother and little sisters.

The year after Mr. Cody's death was a hard one. The Codys' only food was the vegetables from their garden and the animals Billy could trap or shoot.

Finally Billy said to his mother, "Mother, we need money. You and the girls need clothes. We all need more food. I've got to get a job. I'm going to ask Uncle Aleck for work on a wagon train."

Wagon Train Adventures

"Please, Uncle Aleck, won't you let me work in one of your wagon trains?"

Mr. Majors, Uncle Aleck to the Cody children, looked at tall eleven-year-old Billy. "I need men, not boys," said Mr. Majors.

"Yes, but I'm strong. And I can ride. Look!" Billy jumped on a nearby mule and raced around twice in a circle. Then he dropped off the mule's back at Mr. Majors' feet.

Mr. Majors laughed. "You certainly can ride," he said. "You always could. Well, I'll try you as a messenger. The pay is 40 dollars a month. But you'll have to get your mother's consent."

Billy raced home in great excitement. He told his mother he'd send her all the money he earned. Mrs. Cody was sad, but she gave her consent.

Billy ran back to Mr. Majors.

"Good," said Mr. Majors. "First you must take the Wagoner's Oath. Listen carefully." He pulled a paper from his pocket and read:

> I promise not to swear,
> I promise not to drink whisky,
> I promise not to gamble,
> I promise not to be cruel to animals.

When a wagon train stopped for the night, it was a
time for the sharing of food, stories, and fun.

"Do you promise all this?" Mr. Majors asked Billy.
"I promise," said the boy.
"Then sign your name, and you will be a wagoner."
Billy signed with an X. He could not write well.

At dawn the next day Billy was on his mule beside
the wagon train. The long whips of the drivers snapped
like pistols. The oxen bent forward and pulled. They
were off.

Day after day the wagons creaked along over the
dusty plain. Usually they covered fifteen miles each
day. Billy, on his mule, carried messages along the
five-mile line of wagons.

At night the men told stories while they sat around
the campfires. Billy loved it all!

But there were dangers. One day a herd of wild buffalo ran into the train. Some of the oxen broke loose and ran off with the buffalo.

Another time the men heard shots and the galloping of horses' hooves.

"Indians!" yelled their leader. "Leave the wagons. Run to the dry riverbed. Hide behind the banks."

The men raced for the riverbed. Billy tried hard to keep up with them. But he had to stop to rest. Suddenly, against the rising moon, he saw a Sioux brave. Billy raised his gun and fired. The Indian fell.

Two of the wagoners came running back. "Are you safe, Billy?" they asked.

"Oh, yes," said Billy. He told them what had happened. "Did I do right?"

"You did just right," they said. Then one shouted, "Billy killed an Indian all by himself!"

On another trip the wagoners were attacked by a mob of white men. These men stole the guns and bullets. They took all the wagons but one. That wagon was filled with supplies. Then the men and Billy had to walk beside it back to Fort Leavenworth. They walked 1,000 miles!

Billy worked on wagon trains for three years. Then his mother made him leave the plains and come home. His mother had been a schoolteacher. She wanted Billy to go to school.

Snowed In

That winter it snowed and snowed. One day Bill's friend, Dave Harrington, burst into the house.

"Bill, let's go trapping," he said. "I know a place to go where we can find hundreds of beavers. Their skins are worth four dollars apiece."

Fourteen-year-old Bill jumped up; he was eager to go. They got a wagon and two oxen, blankets, food, ammunition, and traps. They took a Bible, too, and other books.

They drove 200 miles in the snow. One morning they saw the paw prints of small animals all around them.

"They are beaver tracks," said Dave, and he stopped the oxen.

The boys built a dugout on the side of a hill. They made a roof, a fireplace, and a chimney. Then they set their traps and waited.

For a while, all went well. They caught many beavers. They skinned them and salted the skins.

Then one of the oxen fell and broke his hip. He had to be shot because he was in such pain.

A few nights later, the boys were awakened by a terrible noise. Dave ran out of the dugout and saw a huge bear killing the other ox. He fired. The wounded bear turned and attacked Dave. Bill rolled out of bed, grabbed his gun, and fired in the dark. He shot the bear and saved Dave's life.

They had no oxen now. But trapping was so good that they decided to stay there until spring.

One day a herd of elk raced by. Bill started after them. But he slipped and fell. He broke his leg.

Dave carried Bill back to the dugout. He set Bill's leg. He made a bed of blankets and animal skins. Then he had to go for help. They had to have oxen to get home.

Dave put firewood near Bill's bed. He put food and books within reach.

"I hate to leave you, Bill," he said. "But I'll be back in 20 days."

Then he started on his hike of 120 miles.

Day after day Bill lay on the bed. He read; he cut notches in a stick, one for each day, and he kept up the fire.

One morning he felt a hand on his head. He thought it was Dave. But he looked up and saw the frowning face of a Sioux Indian. Other Indians came into the dugout. Then their chief entered. Bill knew he was Chief Rain-in-the-Face. Bill used to play with his children.

The chief said, "We came to kill you, to take all your things. But I know you. You will live. My young men will take only your food and your guns."

"But what shall I eat then?" Bill asked the chief.

"This." The chief pointed to a piece of salted elk hanging from the roof. Then the Indians left.

From that day Bill lived only on water and elk meat.

Then came a blizzard. The snow blew down the chimney and crept in around the door. Soon Bill was snowed in. The wolves howled outside the door. Where was Dave?

Days passed. Bill cut a notch for the twenty-seventh day. His meat was all gone now.

The twenty-eighth day came. Another notch. It was very cold. Bill had to burn his last piece of fire-wood. He lay quietly on his bed, wondering how long he could live. He read his Bible. He prayed that God would take care of his mother and little sisters. He did not think of himself. He was not afraid to die.

"Whoa!" someone yelled from outside. "Bill! Bill! I'm here!"

The snow blocking the doorway was pushed aside. Dave had come back. He said that he had been lost in the big snowstorm.

Quickly he built the fire and cooked a good meal. Then he made a bed for Bill in the wagon.

The next day Dave and Bill started home. They were glad that they both were alive. And they felt rich—they had over 400 fine skins.

Riding with the Pony Express

```
WANTED

YOUNG, SKINNY, WIRY FELLOWS,
NOT OVER 16. MUST
BE WILLING TO FACE DEATH
DAILY. WAGES $25 A WEEK.
APPLY CENTRAL OVERLAND
PONY EXPRESS
```

In 1860, signs like this appeared all over the country. The Overland Pony Express was the name for the new, fast mail service. It went from Missouri to California.

Up to this time, mail had been carried by slow stagecoaches. There were no trains yet west of the Mississippi.

Every boy who could ride wanted to join the Pony Express. How excited Bill was when they hired him!

The Pony Express had more than 400 fast horses and 80 riders. The mail was wrapped in waterproof paper to keep it dry. The horses and riders had to cross rivers. They had to ride through rain or snow. They even had to climb two mountain ranges.

Bill Cody rode 45 miles. Then another rider carried the mail on farther. The 45 miles were divided into relays of 15 miles each. A man with a fresh horse was waiting for Bill at every relay post.

The work was dangerous. One day Bill was attacked by fifteen Indians. He dug his spurs into his horse's sides. He lay flat on the horse's back. The pony ran like the wind, and Bill got away without harm.

Later, the Pony Express found that many of the ponies were disappearing. Wild Bill Hickok, a famous scout and an Express rider, thought the Indians had stolen them. He planned a night attack on a nearby Indian village. Bill and a band of men went with him.

They crept up quietly and found the Indians asleep. Suddenly they shot off their guns. The Indians were taken by surprise. All of them surrendered. The men found many of the missing Pony Express horses in the Indians' camp. They took the horses and some Indian ponies back with them.

Once a large sum of money was to be sent in the mail. The company asked for volunteers. Some robbers had already killed one rider who they thought had the money.

Bill Cody offered to take the money through. He was held up by one gang. But he escaped on his fast pony. Later, two men stopped him with six-shooters.

"We know you, Bill," one of them said. "We know you've got the money. Hand over that pouch."

Bill had two pouches with him. He had filled one with waste paper. He threw this pouch hard at one of the men and shot him in the arm. Then he ran his horse into the second robber.

Before the first man could shoot, Bill was well on his way. He carried the money through to his station. He rode over 300 miles without stopping to rest.

The work was hard, too hard for a fifteen-year-old. Night after night, Bill fell into bed, too tired to take off his clothes.

Even at the beginning of the Pony Express, telegraph poles and wires were spelling its end.

The Pony Express was very famous. But it lasted only a few months. Soon there was no need for it. Telegraph poles were springing up all through the West. Telegraph wires could carry messages much faster than horses could.

After his work with the Pony Express, Bill Cody went home. He wanted to see his mother and little sisters.

The Army Scout

At this time there was war between the Northern and the Southern states. Bill Cody wanted to join the Northern, or Union, army. But his mother was sick. She asked him not to go away while she was alive.

Bill's mother lived only a short time after this. Then Bill joined the Union army. General A. J. Smith was Bill's commander.

The general sent for Bill. He saw before him a strong, fine looking young man of eighteen.

"Cody," the general said, "I want you to be an army scout. Do you think you can speak like a Southerner?"

"Yes, sir," said Bill.

"Then dress like a poor farm boy. Get an old farm horse. Go down into Tennessee and mix with the

Southern army. Find out how many soldiers they have. Find out what their plans are. Can you do this?"

"I can, sir."

"Report to me when you return."

Bill started to leave, but General Smith called him back.

"You know, Cody," he said, "that if you are caught, you may be shot as a spy."

"I know, sir," said Bill. "I am not afraid."

The next evening Bill started out. He wore a patched shirt, faded overalls, and a torn hat. He rode an old farm horse. In the morning he stopped at a house and asked for breakfast. He spoke with a southern accent. Everyone thought he was a poor farm boy.

Soon he came to General Forrest's Southern army. He told the guards that he was looking for his father and his brother. The guards let him by. He talked and ate with the soldiers. He acted surprised to see so many men and guns. Soon he learned the army's plans. Then he left, still looking like a farm boy. When Bill returned north, he reported to General Smith.

General Smith told the soldiers that Bill was to be their guide and scout. The army marched south the next day. Bill, in his farmer's clothes, rode just ahead of them.

Soon Bill came to a beautiful, old southern house. An old lady and her daughter were sitting on the porch. Bill rode up to them.

Before he could say a word, the old lady called out, "Come up here, boy, and hide! You're not safe. The Union army's coming. They'll kill you and burn down the house."

Even as she spoke, the soldiers were coming up the road. The troops marched by. Some of the last soldiers dropped out of line. They started running to the house. They were going to steal anything they could find. Bill stepped down from the porch.

"In the name of General Smith," he shouted, "I order you to leave this house alone. Go back to your troops."

The soldiers obeyed.

The old woman turned to Bill in surprise. "Who are you?" she asked.

Bill told her that he was a scout for the Northern army. Then he said, "These men may steal some chickens. But they will not trouble you or your house."

Bill asked for something to eat. They gave him a wonderful dinner.

The men of the house had been in the woods. Now they came out. They might have killed Bill as a Northern spy. Instead, they thanked him for saving their home and protecting their mother and sister.

Besides scouting, Bill helped the army in other ways. He showed them how the Indians fought without losing men. The Indians did not march in the open in a long line. They shot from behind trees or bushes. They hid behind riverbanks and small hills. In this way, few of their men were killed.

After the war was over, Bill scouted for great generals in the West. He helped Sherman, Sheridan, and Custer fight the Indians. He won a medal for bravery and, later, was made a brigadier general.

Buffalo Bill

Bill Cody was a man now. He was married and had a baby daughter.

Bill still loved life on the plains. But his wife, Louisa, did not want to live in the West. She was afraid of the buffalo and the wild Indians.

To please Louisa, Bill bought a hotel. He called it The Golden Rule Hotel. He invited his sister and some friends to live with him. But he would not let them pay him for anything. Of course, he lost money. And he was lonesome for the wide open country.

At this time the first railroad was being built to

the Pacific coast. The workmen found it hard to get food out on the plains. They needed meat. Bill Cody was the best buffalo hunter in the West. So the railroad hired him to bring in twelve buffalo a day. They paid him 500 dollars a month. Even Louisa was willing to move West for so much money.

Bill killed more than 4,000 buffalo for the railroad. Now he was called "Buffalo Bill." As the railroad workers hammered away, they sang:

> Buffalo Bill, Buffalo Bill,
> Never failed and never will;
> When he shoots, he shoots to kill,
> And the company pays
> the buffalo bill.

Bill had two friends who never failed him. These were Lucretia, his gun, and Brigham, his horse. Lucretia was a real buffalo gun, the very best. Brigham was a clever horse, trained for buffalo hunting. Bill never had to tell him what to do. He knew. Bill rode him bareback.

One day Bill was riding along looking for buffalo. Suddenly he saw a band of Indians only a half mile away. They saw Bill. They waved their guns in the air, jumped on their ponies, and started after him.

Daring hunters like Buffalo Bill risked being trampled when they rode into the midst of a herd.

Bill turned Brigham around. He knew that his only chance was to go faster than the Indians. Brigham outran most of the horses. But one kept coming nearer. Bill quickly stopped Brigham. He took aim and shot the Indian's horse. Then Bill and Brigham raced on.

Suddenly two companies of United States soldiers appeared. The Indians turned and fled when they saw them.

Before Bill worked for the railroad, Louisa had been afraid of buffalo. But now she wanted to kill one herself. First, Bill said, she must learn to shoot. He gave her lessons in shooting at a target.

One day Louisa was ready. Bill put her on Brigham. He tied their little daughter tightly to the saddle in front of her. Then Bill, on another horse, rounded up some buffalo. He stayed nearby, ready to help. One buffalo rushed right at Louisa. She raised her gun and fired. The buffalo fell dead.

"Good shot," yelled Bill.

Then another buffalo came rushing up to her. Louisa was so excited that she couldn't hold her gun steady. She fired, but the shot went wild. So Bill shot and killed the buffalo. All this time the baby was cooing happily. She loved to hunt buffalo too!

But soon there were few buffalo left. Greedy sportsmen shot buffalo just for fun. Many men shot from the windows of trains. They left hundreds of buffalo dying on the plains. The great herds of buffalo got smaller and smaller.

The Indians did not like this. They had used the buffalo meat for food. They had used the buffalo skins for clothes and tents. Now the buffalo were almost all gone. Besides this, the white men had taken the Indians' land. They were pushing the Indians off the plains. The Indians said they would fight if they didn't get their land back.

Buffalo Bill knew how the Indians felt. Many Indians were his friends. But he could do nothing about it.

Hunter, Actor, Indian Fighter

Before long, all the country knew of Buffalo Bill, the great hunter and scout.

Men in the East wanted to meet Bill. Plans were made for a group of them to go West. They would camp with Buffalo Bill and shoot buffalo.

The men went out by train. They took all sorts of fancy things with them. There were carpets for the tents and even greyhounds to chase buffalo!

Bill met them. He was dressed in white leather buckskin. His shirt was bright red, and his horse was pure white.

He took his guests to Camp Cody. This was the first "dude ranch." Here the men dressed well. They lived as comfortably as they did at home, and they had wonderful food.

In the morning Bill awoke his guests at three thirty. Soon they were off hunting. The easterners were good shots. They shot buffalo and elk. They shot wild turkeys for dinner.

More and more guests came to Camp Cody. The most famous was the Grand Duke Alexis of Russia. A big dance was given in Denver for the grand duke. Near midnight, a messenger dashed in.

"Buffalo have been seen in Kit Carson County!" he yelled.

The music stopped. The men ran out of the hall. Soon, still in evening clothes, they were racing their horses after the buffalo.

The grand duke wanted to pay Bill for the fun he had at the camp. But Bill wouldn't take money. Instead, the grand duke gave him a fur coat. Later he gave him some gold cuff links. They were shaped like buffalo and covered with diamonds and rubies.

Meanwhile, newspapers were telling the country about Bill. Many books were written about Bill's adventures. Thousands of people read them. Later, Bill wrote some books himself. They told of the exciting life in the West. Not all the stories were true, but all were interesting.

Although Bill was famous, he was not satisfied. Easterners had come to the West. Now he wanted to take the West to the East. He wanted everyone, especially boys and girls, to see real cowboys, Indians, and buffalo.

Soon he got his chance. A play was written for him. In it, men dressed as Indians did a lot of shooting. But the play was not good. Buffalo Bill never learned his lines very well, and the other men did not look or act like real Indians.

Three years later the government called Bill back from the theater. It wanted his help again, to fight against the Indians.

The Sioux and the Cheyenne tribes were on the warpath. The Sioux had never given in to the white men. Now they were led by a great chief, Sitting Bull. They won battle after battle against the United States Army.

At last Sitting Bull set a trap for the white men. General Custer was in charge of the government troops. He rushed right into the chief's trap. The Indians were waiting for him. They killed Custer and all his men.

When Buffalo Bill heard about this, he was very angry. Custer had been his friend. Bill went with the army to fight the Indians.

He saw hundreds of Cheyennes on the edge of the plain. They were riding toward him. But, close by, was one Indian, alone.

Bill and the Indian fired at each other. Bill shot the Indian through the leg and killed his horse. The Indian's bullet went wild.

Just at that moment Bill's horse stumbled and fell. Bill leaped to the ground, faced the Indian, and shot him.

"First scalp for Custer," he shouted, holding up the Indian's warbonnet.

The saying was repeated in the newspapers. The fight was described in different ways, but Bill was always the hero.

The Wild West Show

For years Buffalo Bill had wanted a Wild West Show. He wanted people everywhere to know and love the West as he did.

It was not easy to start such a show. He had to have money; he had to collect and train wild horses. Furthermore, he had to have buffalo, and he needed Indians and sharpshooters.

Finally, with the help of friends, Bill got the show ready. It traveled all over the United States.

What excitement there was when the long gold and white show train came to town! Crowds met it at the railway station. "Buffalo Bill's Wild West Show, Congress of Rough Riders," the sign said.

Buffalo Bill got out first. He was tall and handsome. His light brown hair fell to his shoulders. He took off his big western hat and waved it.

"Hurrah for Buffalo Bill!" yelled the crowd.

Buffalo Bill smiled and waved again. Then little Annie Oakley appeared. She was the best woman sharpshooter in the world.

Next the Indians got off the train. The Indian braves carried their rolled-up tents and their bows and arrows. Their wives carried the pots for cooking. Many Indian women had their babies tied to their backs.

153

Then the cowboys drove out the cattle. "Make way," they kept yelling as the buffalo walked down the gangplank.

Soon the animals were in line, and a parade started. It went down Main Street to the circus grounds. Boys came to watch the tent go up. How they longed to see the show!

"Got enough money for the tickets?" Buffalo Bill would ask them.

Often the answer was "no." Then Buffalo Bill did his best to find them jobs. He paid the boys to put show posters in all the shop windows. One night Tommy and Jimmy were the lucky boys. They had free seats in the front row!

Suddenly the trumpets blew. Buffalo Bill rode in on his horse Charlie. The best actors were with him. They rode to the grandstand and stopped in front of the boys. The horses bowed, pranced, and reared. Then they left quickly.

Next Annie Oakley rode in alone and began shooting. She hit still and moving targets. Then she shot from her galloping horse. She broke glass balls thrown high into the air. The balls came faster and faster, and at last she moved so fast everything seemed blurred. The crowd loved her.

Then cowboys, Mexicans, and Indians came galloping in. They did trick riding. They jumped from

Pretty Annie Oakley—the best woman sharpshooter
in the world and a star of Bill's Wild West Show

the back of one animal to another. Buffalo were let loose, and there was a real buffalo hunt. Next came Indian war dances.

Then the great stage was cleared. In silence the Deadwood Coach appeared, drawn by six horses. The driver drew up in front of the grandstand.

"Is there anyone in the audience who would like to ride in the Deadwood Coach?"

Quick as a flash Tommy jumped up. "I would," he said.

"You will be attacked by Indians!"

But Tommy had already jumped over the railing. He climbed onto the high seat beside the driver.

"Hold on to me," the driver said.

The stagecoach filled with passengers. Then the driver cracked his long whip. The horses jumped ahead. Around the arena they went, faster and faster. Indians appeared. They whooped their war cry; they shot at the stagecoach. One Indian fired at Tommy, but Tommy wasn't hurt.

Suddenly Buffalo Bill and his cowboys dashed through an opening. They fired on the Indians. A horse was hurt. Two Indians fell. The other Indians had had enough, and they rode away.

Buffalo Bill opened the coach door. He bowed as the people came out. Then he looked up at Tommy perched high on the driver's seat.

"Did you have an exciting ride, son?" he asked.

"Oh, yes, sir," said Tommy.

"Then here's something to help you remember it."

He tossed up a shiny silver dollar. Before Tommy could thank him, he had galloped away.

The rest of the show went quickly. Bronco busters came out. Cowboys rode steers, buffalo, and even elk. They roped the animals and tamed them.

Then came Buffalo Bill's fight with Yellow Hand. This fight was made more exciting than it really had been. Buffalo Bill and the tall Indian came from opposite sides of the arena. Slowly they walked toward each other. They fought with guns, then spears. Finally they used knives. Back and forth they went. Suddenly Bill buried his knife in Yellow Hand.

He held up the Indian's scalp lock and shouted, "First scalp for Custer!"

The Indian was carried out. Buffalo Bill bowed low to the cheering crowd.

Of course, no one was really killed. The arrows were rubber tipped, and the scalp lock was a make-believe one. It was all a show with trained actors.

After it was over, people stood on their seats and cheered until they were hoarse.

"Buffalo Bill! Buffalo Bill!" they yelled.

In all America there has never been anything as thrilling as Buffalo Bill's Wild West Show.

Buffalo Bill poses with Sioux Chief Sitting Bull who,
for a time, thrilled audiences in the Wild West Show.

The Show Travels to Europe

All Europe wanted to see the Wild West Show. Bill decided to take it across the Atlantic Ocean.

In London the show grounds were very large, so Buffalo Bill showed the English some real Indian life.

The stage lights were dim to make it look like dawn. The Indians were asleep in their tepees. Wild animals roamed about. Then the sky brightened. The Indians awoke, and they came out of their tepees. They danced a war dance. Suddenly a lookout raced into the arena.

"Enemy coming!" he yelled. "On the warpath!"

The Indians grabbed their weapons. Almost at once enemy Indians were upon them. They waved spears and bows and arrows. With loud war whoops they attacked the Indians in the village. Men and horses were shot. But as the sun rose, the attackers were driven off.

Then came a make-believe windstorm. It blew the Indian village right off the stage. The audience loved this.

There was a buffalo hunt too. Buffalo Bill showed the English his own way of shooting buffalo. He never missed.

Queen Victoria of England came to the show. When Buffalo Bill rode in on his horse Charlie, he stopped before the queen's box. Charlie knelt down. A soldier dipped an American flag three times before the queen. The queen stood and saluted the flag. How the crowd cheered!

"America!" they yelled. "America and England."

The queen invited Bill to bring the show to Windsor Palace. There four visiting kings rode in Bill's stagecoach. A crown prince sat with the driver.

After London, the show went to Paris. Hundreds of artists came to paint the Indians and cowboys.

In Italy, Buffalo Bill promised that his cowboys would tame any horse brought to them. Dangerous horses were brought from all over the country. One Italian duke turned two of his wild horses loose in the arena. The wild horses jumped up in the air. They bucked; they twisted. But the cowboys lassoed them. They tied them between two trained horses. In five minutes they had the wild horses saddled and were riding them.

For several years the Wild West Show visited Europe. It played to cheering crowds wherever it went.

Memories of Buffalo Bill

The most exciting Wild West Show was held in Chicago in 1893. Bill had invited riders from all over

This poster advertised Bill's "rough riders" of many nations.

the world. Cossacks came from Russia with their wild ponies. Swift Arabian horses were brought from northern Africa. Men of different nations raced each other.

Best of all, Buffalo Bill invited 15,000 children to come to the show—FREE. Before they left, they were given ice cream and candy.

After Chicago there were more shows. Then accidents began to happen. In one town the big tent burned. In another, a grandstand fell to the ground. Then the show train was hit in a railroad crash. Annie Oakley was badly hurt.

161

Bill had money troubles too. He had made millions of dollars. But he had spent them too easily. Also he had trusted the wrong men. He had to sell part of the show to a circus.

Bill was growing old. He was often very tired. Finally he became sick. But he still appeared in every show. He wouldn't disappoint his audience who loved him.

Buffalo Bill Cody died in 1917. He was buried on Lookout Mountain, about 20 miles from Denver, Colorado. Eighteen thousand people marched in bitter cold to his funeral.

People who go West like to visit the fine Buffalo Bill Museum in Cody, Wyoming. Bill's medals, his trophies, and his guns are there.

Tourists also look up to the hill between Rattlesnake Mountain and Cedar Mountain. There, against the Wyoming sky, they see a great bronze statue of Buffalo Bill. It was built with pennies from children all over the United States. Bill sits high on his horse, reining him in. His gun is raised in his right hand. He is looking out over the plains. Perhaps he sees a herd of buffalo. Perhaps his keen eyes sight Indians on the warpath.

Index

A

Alexis, Grand Duke, 150, 151
Arapaho Indians, 114, 115
Arikara Indians, 19, 20, 22, 56
Ashley, William Henry, 15, 18, 19, 21, 27, 54, 55
Assiniboine Indians, 56

B

Bannock Indians, 68, 69
Baptiste (trapper), 22
Bear Lake, 27, 32, 66
Bear River, 64, 66, 68
Beaver, 17, 58–60, 75, 102 (pic), 103, 104, 137
Bent, Charles, 96, 97, 98, 99, 100, 105, 107, 119
Bent's Fort, 106, 107 (pic), 118
Bent's Trading Post, 106, 109
Big Horn Mountains, 17
Black, Art, 15, 24, 27, 37
Blackfoot Indians, 17–18, 43 (pic), 71, 72, 118
Black Whiteman (Cheyenne), 106, 107, 108, 109
Bodmer, Charles, 42
   paintings of
      Beaver Lodge on the Missouri, 102
      Fort McKenzie with the Combat of Twenty-Eighth of August, 1833, 44
      Junction of the Yellowstone River with the Missouri, 58
      Pehriska-Ruhpa, 45
Bridger, Cora (wife of Jim Bridger), 74, 75, 78
Bridger, James (Jim), 47 (pic)
   as army scout, 79–80
   and Ashley expedition, 55–56, 58
   and Bannock Indians, 68–70
   and Bear River, 64–66
   and Blackfoot Indians, 71–73
   as blacksmith, 52, 53, 60, 76
   childhood of, 49, 50 (pic), 51, 52
   and Crow Indians, 61
   death of, 81

and father, 49, 51, 52
   as ferry operator, 51, 52
   and Fort Bridger, 76, 77 (pic), 79
   at Great Salt Lake, 64–67, 128
   and Jed Smith, 61
   and Kit Carson, 105, 114, 115
   and mother, 51, 52
   at South Pass, 63
   as storyteller, 87, 126
   in Yellowstone country, 67, 74
   as young trapper, 55, 56, 58, 60
Bridger, Mary Ann (daughter of Jim Bridger), 75, 76, 78
Bridger, Virginia (daughter of Jim Bridger), 79, 81
Buffalo, 43 (pic), 82 (pic), 83–84, 99, 147, 148 (pic), 149, 150, 154, 157, 159
Buffalo Bill. *See* Cody, William F.
Buffalo Bill Museum (Wyoming), 162

C

California, 27, 29, 30, 32, 35, 41, 75, 78, 105, 140
Camp Cody, 150–151
Carson, Adaline (daughter of Kit Carson), 118, 119
Carson, Becky (mother of Kit Carson), 90, 91, 94, 95
Carson, Big Mose (brother of Kit Carson), 93
Carson, Christopher (Kit), 89 (pic)
   as apprentice saddlemaker, 94, 97
   and Charles Bent, 96, 97, 98–100, 105, 107, 119
   and Bent's Fort, 106, 107 (pic), 118
   and Cheyenne Indians, 109
   childhood of, 90–91, 92 (pic), 93–94
   in Civil War, 122
   and Crow Indians, 106–109
   death of, 123
   and death of father, 93–94
   as explorer, 121
   and Frémont, 119, 120 (pic), 121
   and grizzly bears, 111–114

163